"BAD TEACHERS is good news for parents. Guy Strickland brings an insider's insights to the tricky task of interpreting kids' signals about teacher trouble—and offers innovative, on-target solutions to a pervasive problem."

—TAMARA EBERLEIN,
author of *Whining: Tactics for Taming Demanding Behavior*

Does this sound familiar?

Amanda has a recurring case of the "Seven-thirty Stomachache." Odd, how it never happens on weekends or holidays. . . .

Steven used to come home and tell you all about his day in school. Now, he doesn't volunteer anything except short answers.

After school, Ronny needs to burn up his wild bursts of energy. Stay out of his way, and turn him loose for about a half hour, and then he is okay.

Caroline does her homework easily, but only after you have explained it to her. If she ever got an explanation in school, it must have gone right over her head.

Bad attitude, low grades, poor behavior—they can make every child's schooling unhappy and unproductive. What if the problem isn't with your kids, but with your kids' *teachers?* Now, this authoritative book shows how you can become an advocate for your children's education, and protect their spirit, mind, *and* future from

BAD TEACHERS

BAD

TEACHERS

The Essential Guide for Concerned Parents

Guy Strickland

POCKET BOOKS

New York   London   Toronto   Sydney   Tokyo   Singapore

An *Original* Publication of POCKET BOOKS

POCKET BOOKS, a division of Simon & Schuster Inc.
1230 Avenue of the Americas, New York, NY 10020

Strickland, Guy.
    Bad teachers / Guy Strickland.
        p.   cm.
    Includes bibliographical references.
    ISBN 0-671-52934-X
    1. Teacher effectiveness—United States.   2. Teachers—Rating of—
United States.   3. Teacher-student relationships—United States.
I. Title.
LB1775.2.S77   1998
371.102'3—dc21   97-41482
                                                                      CIP

First Pocket Books trade paperback printing March 1998

10   9   8   7   6   5   4   3   2

POCKET and colophon are registered trademarks of Simon & Schuster Inc.

Text design by Stanley S. Drate/Folio Graphics Co. Inc.
Cover design by Claudia Acunto
Cover photo by Andrea Burns

Printed in the U.S.A.

*To the many teachers
who made this book possible
and the few who make it necessary*

Acknowledgments

To Williams College, where I learned to doubt the conventional wisdom.

To the Graduate School of Education at UCLA, where I learned the conventional wisdom, and doubted it.

To all the children whom I have taught, and from whom I have learned so much.

To my wife, who showed exceptional patience over the years it took to write this book.

To Carol Mann, an exceptional agent, who saw the value of the message and presented it so well.

To Leslie Stern, who did a superb job of polishing it for the reader.

Most especially to Barbara Lagowski, who took a raw work and reorganized it to make it readable. She guided me paragraph by paragraph through the rewriting process, and she helped make these ideas accessible to the reader. Every page of this book bears the stamp of her hand.

Contents

PART THREE

PRIVATE SCHOOLS AND
PERSONAL SOLUTIONS

Introduction:
Leveling the Playing Field

"Once upon a time, Sarah loved school; she used to come home and set up all her dolls as a classroom, with herself as the teacher. Now she doesn't even want to go to school. Sometimes I have to go in with her, just to get her there."

"Tommy's having a bad year. His grades are down, and he says he doesn't understand the work. The teacher keeps saying that he needs to study harder, but that doesn't seem to help."

"I had to go talk to the teacher again about Jack. He's always been such a good boy, but now he keeps getting in trouble. I don't understand it—he's well behaved at home."

Elementary school children are the joys of our lives, with smiles that warm the room. They still believe in a world of fairness and kindness. They try very hard to please their parents and teachers, and try very hard to get along with their friends. Because they try so hard to be good, they are surprised and bewildered when things go badly at school.

Low grades, bad behavior, bad attitude: These are all problems that can make a child's life unhappy. And since any pain in your child becomes your pain, too, you want to dig out the causes and solve the problem. The school will blithely tell you what causes your child's problem;

1

they will tell you that it is his lack of effort, lack of control, or lack of intelligence.

Maybe.

Maybe not.

Maybe the problem doesn't lie within your child at all. There is another common source of educational problems like these, and it's a source you won't hear about from the principal, the superintendent of schools, the school board, or the teacher: the bad teacher.

Before we consider the bad teachers, we need to put things in perspective: Thank Heaven for the good teachers! We are grateful for the people who have dedicated their lives to opening the world for our children. We appreciate the work they do and the grueling conditions they endure. As we all know, teaching small children pays poorly, requires long hours, and commands no respect, so we wouldn't want to do it ourselves. But we are grateful that others are willing to do the work.

How do we show our gratitude? We honor the teachers with awards, newspaper articles, plaques from the First Lady, shows on the Disney Channel, or maybe even a slot in the astronaut program. We give them lots of honors because it's cheaper than paying them what they are worth. We compare their salaries to the salaries of entertainers and sports stars, and shake our heads. Teachers aren't paid enough, we say, and then we complain to the city council about the education budget.

We are indoctrinated with the idea that all teachers are selfless and dedicated, yielding their own personal benefit for the good of the community. That's the official line, and there's a lot of truth in it if you don't look too closely. The school district pushes the official line because homage is cheaper than other fringe benefits. The teacher union pushes the official line because it's a good argument for pay raises and improved teaching conditions. The newspaper pushes the official line because it makes good "human interest" stories. But there are several problems with the official line.

The truth is, teachers are underpaid. But on the other hand, the vacations are excellent, the working conditions are generally clean and good, and the pay is sufficient to match supply with demand.

The bigger problem with the official line is that not all teachers are selfless and dedicated. And some are selfless and dedicated but incompetent. Teaching, like any other profession, includes people of varying ability, from the excellent to the execrable.

Most teachers are nurturing, self-sacrificing, and inspiring, but it would be naive to pretend that they all are. Some are indifferent, some are incompetent, and a few are downright destructive. Best estimates indicate that 5 to 15 percent of teachers fall into the "incompetent" category. That means that, of the one million elementary schoolteachers in the country, 50,000 to 150,000 are bad teachers. At twenty children per class, at least one to three million children have to suffer with a bad teacher each year; and it's a different one to three million each year.

In short, there *are* bad teachers, and they are found in public and private schools, in highly paid positions as well as the poorest school districts. It is quite likely that, sooner or later, one of them will be in your child's classroom.

In thirty years as an educator, I've seen bad teachers in every kind of educational setting and at all levels. As much as it pains me to admit it, there was a time when I

saw a bad teacher with each glance at the mirror. When
I first began teaching, I knew nothing about learning disabilities. There were kids I couldn't reach, and I didn't
know why. So I blamed it on the kids; those who weren't
"getting it" were dumb, or obstinate, or rowdy. Gradually
I figured out that if the child exhibited learning or behavior problems in the classroom, there was always a reason;
and since all kids really want to succeed, the reason was
invariably something beyond the child's control. The
more I learned about my students and their learning
styles, the better the kids became. And the more I learned,
the more I was forced to confront the truth: When I had
blamed the children, I was compounding their problems
rather than solving them. I became aware of the bad
teacher I had been, and conscious of the effects that previous bad teachers had on my current students.

As a teacher, I have taught entire classes damaged by
a bad teacher's ignorance and insensitivity. As a school
principal, I've had to retrain bad teachers and try to get
rid of them (a nearly impossible proposition). Now, as an
educational consultant, I work individually with students to patch up the damage of bad teaching. I've seen
small boys punished for acting like small boys, children
who haven't learned math because the teacher never
taught any, children who struggle hopelessly because the
teachers never recognized obvious learning disabilities.
And year after year, I've seen parents whose children
have been injured by incompetent, uncaring, or overly
controlling teachers, searching without benefit of training or even encouragement for a solution to their children's educational problems—or a way to mend their
battered psyches.

For the parents who want to do something about their

child's bad teacher, there have been no books, no articles, and no useful advice—until now. Since all of the advice in print was written by educators, not parents, the issue of teacher incompetence was rarely addressed. When it was, the parent was never offered guidance, just self-serving platitudes like, "Wait till next year. . . . Your child will catch up. . . . Your child can't change his teacher any more than he or she will be able to choose his boss in adult life. . . . Consider it a life lesson and endure." This is excellent advice if your goal is to protect the bad teacher, make life easier for the school administrators, and perpetuate the problem. But if you need to save your own child from the bad teacher who is trampling her ego and undermining her competency *now*, you need much better advice.

I wrote this book to provide parents with that much-needed advice. Until now, defending one's child against a bad teacher has been a battle with unfair odds. The entire entrenched school bureaucracy defends its incompetent teachers with a myriad of weapons, including codes of silence, labor unions and contracts, stonewalling, and stalling maneuvers. The poor victimized child's only allies have been his parents, who have never fought before and don't really want to fight at all. The parents are completely unarmed and are unaware of the weapons arrayed against them. It's no surprise that aggrieved parents usually give up quickly and that year after year, the children lose.

The bad news is that the administrators of your child's school won't make it easy for you to save your child from his bad teacher. The good news is that this book will help you. This book will tell you:

- How to identify good and bad teachers
- How to avoid assignment to bad teachers
- How to make sure the problem is the teacher
- How to make the most of teacher conferences
- What to say to the principal to get your child the attention he deserves
- What *not* to say to the principal if you want action
- And how, if all else fails, to help your child survive a bad teacher.

These strategies have worked for hundreds of families, and they can work for your family, too.

Too many children have had their fragile egos battered, their curiosity smothered, and their enthusiasm destroyed by bad teachers. No child should have to go through that. You have raised your child with fairness and kindness, and you expect schools to do the same. When they fail, you are the only defender of your child; you are the only voice demanding fairness and kindness for your child. With this book, you will be able to stand up for your child and protect his spirit and mind from the bad teachers.

PART ONE

IDENTIFYING

THE

PROBLEM

1

Trouble at
Water Street School

You are dropping your son Johnny off at school, as you always do. Getting out of the car, he pauses. "Oh, here," he says as an afterthought, and tosses you a crumpled envelope. He is through the schoolhouse door before you have a chance to open the envelope.

You know what it is anyway; you've been expecting it for some time now. It's a summons from Johnny's teacher requesting that you attend a conference. Johnny knows what it is, too; that's why he staged the delivery of the note as an exit line. He didn't want to listen to your lecture, or start his morning with a grilling from you.

Johnny is having trouble at school, and he assumes from past experiences that it's his own fault. He's all boy, and that rowdiness sometimes spills over into the classroom. Ever since he was little, you have seen him set his little jaw and put on that "I'm determined to be naughty" look. It would be surprising if he never did that in class. As a toddler, Johnny would shake the playpen to see if it was firm enough to hold him. Now he's always testing the rules to see if they are firm. Perhaps if you had been more strict, he would exert more self-control in the classroom. But he is only eight years old, and you are only partway through the on-the-job training program known as parenthood.

All in all, you know you are a good parent. You have invested enormous time and effort to help Johnny grow up straight, strong, and full of intellectual curiosity. You've helped him learn to get along with other kids, you've read to him and taught him to love books and look forward to his first day of school. When you couldn't be there yourself, you enrolled him in the best day care and preschools available. You coddled him and paddled him, sometimes more than necessary and sometimes on the wrong occasions; you did the best you could, not always perfectly but always with love. And like all good parents, you wondered constantly, "Did I do enough? Did I do too much? Did I do it the right way?" You won't know for forty more years, until you see how Johnny's own kids turn out.

But in the meantime, Johnny's in trouble at school right now, and Johnny assumes it's his own fault. You assume that the fault is Johnny's, or possibly your own. Maybe you are both at fault . . . or maybe not?

Johnny's Failing Math.
Is Someone Failing Johnny?

You sit there in your car, watch Johnny flee into the schoolhouse, and then open the summons. It's a short, polite note asking you to call the school secretary to schedule "a meeting to discuss Johnny's work and behavior." There are no clues here saying exactly what the teacher wants to talk about, because the teacher doesn't want you to come to the meeting prepared. But you have to assume the teacher has bad things to say. You exhale deeply, shift gears, and pull into the traffic.

As you drive away, you wonder whatever happened to the bright-eyed kindergartner, full of enthusiasm and curiosity about the world around him, whom you delivered to these doors not so very long ago. When did the fire go out? When did mornings become such a struggle and Mondays become such agony? So much has been lost since the day he started at Water Street School.

Water Street is like most schools—not a bad school. It's the basic neighborhood school that all the local kids attend. Its ethnic and economic diversity reflects the streets around it. Some of the children's parents are also graduates of the school. Water Street School is a community "fixture."

You are a realistic parent. You send your child to Water Street School knowing that he may not grow up to be president or a rocket scientist or a doctor or a lawyer; you simply want your child to become the best that he can be. You want him to be enthusiastic, self-confident, and interested in learning so that when he finds his dream he will have the tools to achieve it.

But so far, that doesn't seem to be happening at Water Street. You know you need to do something to help your child, but you aren't sure where the problem lies. Does it lie with Johnny? When he is engaged in an activity that interests him, he works enthusiastically and with boundless interest—the way you wish he did in school. So maybe Johnny is fine, and the problem is in the school or the teachers.

Water Street School has some excellent teachers, underpaid but devoted people who are selflessly giving their lives for our children. But it would be naive to assume that every teacher at Water Street is a Mother Teresa; in a typical school like Water Street, 15 to 30 percent of the teachers are in some way inadequate. Five percent are actually damaging children, and they should quit or be fired immediately (estimates based on a study by the American Association of School Administrators).

It's surprising how many good teachers there are at Water Street, if you think about the odds against good teaching:

- For a college graduate, most other jobs pay better.
- There is no career path: that is, there are very few chances for advancement. So the most capable and ambitious people leave teaching for more rewarding careers.
- The teacher's boss judges her not on how well she teaches, but on how well and how quietly she manages her classroom, so there is no incentive to teach well.
- A teacher's pay scale is based not on how well he teaches but on his years of experience and number of postcollege credits, so there is no incentive to excel.
- Teachers discover that if they really want to teach, they are almost alone; most teachers and school administrators have their own goals that take precedence over student achievement.
- Public school teachers can't be fired for anything short of a felony conviction, so there is no real incentive to teach well, or even adequately.

The school structure seems to ensure that bad teachers stay in teaching. School principals routinely give them inflated performance evaluations and carefully conceal from parents any evidence that the school has any bad teachers. (Chapter 8 will reveal more about how and why the principal protects the incompetent teacher.)

Nor is the principal the only—or the most powerful—defender of the bad teacher. Laws and labor unions protect teachers, competent or otherwise, from any accountability for their performance. If class after class of students learn nothing, then the teacher may be incompetent in your eyes—but not according to the law. In the legal definition of incompetence, the children are irrelevant.

School districts shuffle the bad teachers around, because they don't want to exert the effort or expend the resources it would take to fire them. School district personnel, like every one else in education, have priorities of their own: cost control, maintaining the district's reputation (and their own reputations), responding to political pressures, etc. Whether your child learns anything is a very low priority. This will also be discussed in greater detail in the chapters that follow.

You know a number of parents, at Water Street School and elsewhere, who have tried to blame the teachers for their children's problems. Although the complaints were justified, the teachers were never compelled to accept responsibility for their failings. Parents who complain, however politely, find that blame flows like water, always following the path of least resistance. Since teachers are much more articulate and powerful than children, and much more experienced at shifting the blame away from themselves, the blame ultimately pools at the foot of the child. It's too easy for the parents to blame themselves, or to accept the teacher's assessment that the

child isn't learning because she is "lazy," "underachiev-
ing," "misbehaving," or lacking in some way. Blaming
the victim, or standing silent when the teacher blames
the victim, isn't fair and it isn't constructive, but it is
very easy—and therefore common.

Of course, parents will shoulder as much blame as
they are able to carry, and parents are strong enough to
carry a lot of blame. Age and experience have given us
ways of coping with problems, so we can carry the
weight of the world. But little children can be crushed by
much smaller burdens. When a bad teacher won't accept
responsibility for the child's inadequacy, a whole chain of
events follow: The child thinks of himself as a complete
failure, socially, physically, and mentally; the parents
think of the child as a failure; and the child's classmates
think of him as a failure. Each of these perceptions has
far-reaching negative consequences. It is an appalling
burden for an irresponsible adult to lay on an innocent
child.

When Bad Teachers Happen to Good Kids

Several years ago, a newspaper researched a group of
successful people from one community, seeking to find
out why they had succeeded and others from the same
community had failed. It turned out that the successful
ones had all had the same kindergarten teacher forty
years before. She had instilled in each of them a love of
learning, a love of reading, and a feeling of competence
that made them eager to meet new challenges. This
teacher's actions created an impact on her students, and

their families, and their community, that could still be seen decades later.

Of course, a teacher can also change someone's life for the worse. Nancy, for example, had spent her young life cheerfully doing all that her parents and teachers had asked of her. Then, in only five weeks with an overbearing and unfair teacher, her self-image and her achievement were thoroughly crushed. Stepping in to protect her from this teacher was not enough; it is taking years to repair the damage caused to her love of learning, to her self-concept, and to her reputation among her classmates. It is appalling to consider the impact of a full year with this teacher. Forty years from now, you wonder how many *unsuccessful* people will point to *this* teacher in their backgrounds. I've known hundreds of kids like Nancy who have had their personalities deformed and their lives altered by bad teachers.

The teacher is an extremely important person in a child's life. The child spends more time with this adult, takes more advice from this adult, patterns more of his behavior after this adult, and interacts more with this adult than any other grown-up he'll encounter outside of the home. Clearly, this adult will have a huge influence, for good or evil, on the child.

There is a poster that reads, "A child learns what she lives." If the teacher treats the child with respect, the child will think well of herself. If the teacher treats the child as a capable learner, the child will feel competent. Especially in the lower elementary grades, the child's opinion of herself will be a direct reflection of the teacher's opinion of her. A good teacher can make a child feel confident about herself and her ability. A bad teacher in the lower grades can destroy a child's faith in herself; and a bad teacher in the upper elementary grades can destroy her desire to learn.

Too often, when a child has a bad teacher, the parents do nothing at all. They assume the difficulty is a phase, or a temporary problem; they don't want the unpleasantness of a confrontation; they buy into what teachers have told them and accept the idea that their child is the problem; or they feel that they didn't discover the difficulty early enough and decide to hold on until next year. From an adult's perspective, a year flies by quickly; but a year is nearly 15 percent of a seven-year-old's lifetime. No wonder a year with a bad teacher seems like an eternity in hell to a child. Even a few months is too large a proportion of a child's life to spend adapting to unreasonable demands from an incompetent or unstable teacher, working without guidance or reward, or feeling too small and too inexperienced to protect himself effectively.

Nor is it ever a good idea to let the problem slide, to see if it will go away or get worse. While it is possible that the problem will go away on its own, it's impossible to guess how many straws it will take to break the child's back. How many times can he be called stupid before he believes it? How many times can she be punished before she decides that she might as well make the crime fit the punishment? How many times can he be driven to anger before he becomes an angry child? How many times must a child be labeled before she accepts the label?

And how long does it take for his classmates to start labeling him? They say that, once you get a reputation as an early riser, you can sleep as late as you want. The reputation hangs on long after the reason for it has faded away. If your child gets a reputation as a troublemaker, or a class clown, or a victim, his classmates will treat him that way even if he stops being the troublemaker, clown, or victim. Whatever the reputation, he will either spend years living it down, or waste a lifetime living up to it. The self-fulfilling prophecy is almost a commandment to children. For them, growing up is a process of meeting the expectations of others.

The effects I've outlined here are serious ones, things that can scar a child for life. It's enough to make a loving parent want to run to the phone and schedule that parent-teacher conference as soon as humanly possible. It's a good impulse . . . but it's an impulse that's a bit premature. Hold off on the phone call until you have listened more to your child.

What You Can Learn Only from Your Child

Parent-teacher conferences are a lot like geometry. In geometry, two points define a line. In the conference, if there are only two points of view (yours and the teacher's), all you will get is a line. If you want the plain (plane) truth, you need a third point of view, the child's.

You weren't in school with your child; you don't know what your child has done or has experienced. There's no videotape of her actions or reactions. You are at the mercy of the teacher's description of the events at school.

This means that the teacher is free to edit the description in any way she sees fit. She can omit or revise facts that make her culpable; she can exaggerate facts that serve her purposes; and she can ignore facts that do not support her conclusions. She can get away with it, because you weren't there. She can feed you a line, and you won't know bait from barb.

But if you have taken the time and effort to listen to your child, you can bring that third point of view to the conference. And that third point will give you the plane, the level playing field, that is fair to all the players, where the plain truth comes out.

Unfortunately, children are great perceptors of information but are not great translators of information. This means that, although the child correctly perceives a problem with her teacher, she may translate it as a problem with herself; as a result, it is not always easy to get the real story from a child, particularly one who is young and/or under stress. If your child is upset by a situation at school, her way of communicating with you may be quite subtle. In most cases, the cry for help will need to be decoded and translated.

"My Stomach Hurts!" and Other Signs of Trouble at Water Street School

Amanda has a recurring case of the "Seven-thirty Stomachache." Odd how it never happens on weekends or holidays. . . .

Steven used to come home and tell you all about his day in school. Now he doesn't volunteer anything except short answers.

Jenny used to show you her work, but now she hides it.

After school, Ronny needs to burn up his wild bursts of energy. Stay out of his way, and turn him loose for about a half hour, and then he is okay.

Jeff doesn't know how to get his homework started.

Bill starts strongly on the homework, but can't seem to get it finished. Sometimes he finishes it and then forgets to turn it in.

Caroline does her homework easily, after you have explained it to her. If she ever got an explanation in school, it must have gone right over her head.

Each child here has a message for the parent, that something has gone wrong at school. The child is trying to deal with a situation that is beyond his control. He needs your help, and he doesn't know how to ask you for that help.

Some children spontaneously tell their parents everything, especially girls (who are usually more articulate than boys) and younger children (who are usually more open). Some children will talk about their school day if they are asked the right questions. As children grow older, they are more likely to treat school and home as separate territories—their turf and your turf—that should be kept separate. By the end of elementary school, they may even resent parents "prying" into affairs at their school. It may take some serious effort to extract information about problems with a particular teacher.

In an ideal world, you will already have established open lines of communication with your child. You can discuss all kinds of problems, including school problems, easily and immediately. In the real world, however, your child may have neither the vocabulary nor the understanding to reveal his fears and problems, so you will have to help him communicate. Since the child's viewpoint is critical to any parent-teacher conference, here are three tips to help improve communication with your child and get to the heart of his feelings about the situation:

1. Look at her. Find a time and a place where you are face-to-face, so you can each focus your attention on communicating with each other.

2. Touch him. You can show concern and sympathy much better with touch than with words. Your touch will encourage him to confide in you, and will help keep him focused on the issue at hand. As the child grows older, touching him becomes more difficult, but it also becomes more important.

3. Listen to her. Don't argue, don't contradict, don't edit, just listen. If you want to know what's on her mind, don't put words in her mouth. Ask open-ended questions, not the yes-no variety, and as few as possible. By being a good listener, you can encourage her to talk.

Ask general questions that don't seem too personal or prying. How do the other kids like the teacher? What does the teacher do when the kids don't understand the assignment? What does the teacher do when the kids misbehave a little? Is there a teacher's pet? What does the teacher do while the kids are working? Do the kids think the teacher is fair?

Maintaining open lines of communication with your child is a long-term project. You can't expect your child to be a great talker the first time you decide to be a great listener. So remember: This process may take a while.

When your child begins to reveal his concerns, bear in mind that the things that are very important to a youngster can seem silly to an adult. Why won't the teacher let me keep a stuffed animal in my desk? Can I use the purple pen that Aunt Kate gave me? What if the new teacher won't let us go to the bathroom? Do we have to play kick-ball at recess? Will the kids laugh at my show-and-tell?

When your child expresses these concerns, you want to reassure him that everything will be okay. But the truth is, you don't have control over all these things. In some cases, only the teacher can provide the answers. Your job, as parents, is to convey your child's concerns to the teacher so *he* can reassure your child. Write down the child's questions, in words as close as possible to your child's own words; that way, it will be clear to the teacher that it is a concern of the child rather than a complaint of the parent.

For example, your gentle child may be frightened when the teacher raises his voice. The child thinks that the loud voice represents anger that will be followed by punishment, when in fact it only means "be more orderly when lining up for recess." You understand this, and you are not accusing the teacher of ranting and raving. If you are careful to present your child's side of the story in his own words, then it will be clear that you are expressing concern about the child's perception rather than about the teacher's performance.

At the same time, it will give you an opportunity to gauge the teacher's response. You will find out whether he is receptive to a child's emotional concerns, or whether he treats your comments as criticism. If the teacher feels criticized, it will be interesting to see whether he reacts with anger, indifference, or defensiveness. You may learn a lot about your child's daytime environment when you evaluate the teacher's reactions.

A final note: Always give your child the benefit of the doubt. When she is telling you about her school experiences, she is telling the truth from her point of view. Your superior experience and perspective may tell you that the child has the facts wrong, but that doesn't make the child wrong. The child's observations are a correct and truthful account of how things look from her perspective. And if her perspective causes her fear and concern, then those feelings are also real and true and in need of resolution.

A parent-teacher conference without any input from the child is like a court hearing without the only eyewitness. Any effective parent-teacher conference simply must include the child. He has information and a perspective that neither parent nor teacher can bring to the conference. In the child's absence, the other conferees might agree on what has occurred, but they are merely speculating about why it occurred. And if they don't know what caused the problem, they surely won't know how to resolve it. The child's physical presence may not be required for most of the conference if the parents who are actively representing the child already know the facts and can reliably express the child's point of view.

Preparing for the Conference

Now you are ready to phone the Water Street School secretary to schedule the parent-teacher conference. You will be asked to choose a time and place that is convenient for the teacher. You will also be asked to meet on the teacher's turf—certainly at the school, and probably in her classroom. That way, if the teacher feels the need to produce evidence in her own behalf, she can easily do so. She can also let you know when your time with her is up—whether or not you've had your say.

As you put down the phone and pencil the conference

into your calendar, you think about what might happen there. You have read all the hopeful articles in parents' magazines about constructive parent-teacher conferences, so you know what is *supposed* to happen. You and the teacher are supposed to exchange information pleasantly about Johnny's educational background. Then you are supposed to pinpoint specific problems and plan out a strategy to correct the problems. Together, in a spirit of camaraderie, you will work together to carry out the plan. Johnny will emerge a better student, and then child, parent, and teacher live happily ever after, as in any good fairy tale.

Life isn't always like that. The truth is, those constructive parent-teacher conferences articles were often written by teachers, not by parents, who assume that the teacher in the conference is a qualified superteacher like themselves, who think of teaching as a "calling" rather than a job. They assume that the teacher is all-wise and all-knowing, and that the parent is helpful and cooperative but not too bright. The possibility that the *teacher* may be the problem never occurs to the authors of those articles. Even the possibility that wisdom may sit on both sides of the table is never considered.

You, as a parent, have been your own child's teacher since the day he was born. You know more than anyone else about what inspires him to tune in to a subject, what causes him to tune out, and the way he behaves when bored, stifled, stressed, or happily engaged (some kids are more boisterous when they are happy and interested than when they are not). You assume that your observations will be useful to the teacher. Maybe . . . maybe not. It depends on why the teacher asked for this meeting and what she expects to get from it.

If the teacher views the conference as an opportunity to get more information about Johnny so she can understand him better, your input will be crucial. The teacher may want details about his struggles with homework so she will know how to help him. Or she might ask how he relates to other children outside the classroom, so she can better understand his behavior. Clearly, in this type of conference, the parents make an important contribution that will benefit Johnny and the teacher.

On the other hand, the teacher may have called the conference to present a plan. Perhaps the teacher feels she has already reached an understanding of the problem, and has devised a plan to solve it. In this case, the teacher may have called the meeting to get your approval of the plan, or to secure your cooperation in carrying it out. Since the plan is already a "done deal," your input will be limited.

Another possibility is that the teacher has concocted a plan to solve the problem even though she really doesn't know what the problem is. All the teacher knows is that Johnny is doing badly and it is imperative that she absolve herself of responsibility for his difficulty by *appearing* to do something. By bringing you in on the plan, and co-opting your agreement to it, you can't blame her if the plan doesn't work, because it's your plan, too. Nor can you accuse her of doing nothing in the child's behalf.

A final possible purpose of the meeting may be that the teacher doesn't have a plan at all, and also doesn't understand the problem. She only knows that Johnny is doing badly and that Johnny is going to get a very bad report card. Since every teacher knows that it is a cardinal sin to send home a bad report card with no prior warning, she needs to cover herself by notifying the parents in advance. In effect, then, the purpose of the meeting is for the teacher to make negative observations and comments about Johnny. Having notified you, the teacher feels she has fulfilled her obligation. All you are required to do at the conference, as the teacher sees it, is to feel guilty and embarrassed, and promise to change Johnny's behavior and performance. Later, when the bad report card arrives, you are expected to feel acquiescent while the teacher feels justified.

These are the possible scenarios. You don't know yet what the teacher wants from this conference, but you know what you want. You want the teacher to demonstrate a deep personal knowledge of Johnny. A good teacher shouldn't have to refer to a grade book when asked to point out a student's specific strengths and weaknesses.

You want to find out what Johnny knows or doesn't know. Is he relatively weaker in adding with three-digit numbers, solving word problems, understanding the structure of the number system, distinguishing numerator from denominator? Does he have the same difficulty with other subjects that he has with arithmetic? Is his difficulty the problem—or is it a symptom of a more wide-ranging condition such as a learning disorder?

You want to know what the teacher has to say about Johnny's problems, and how she defines them. After a little prodding, Johnny had a lot to say about the problems as he defined them; you want to see whether the teacher is addressing the same problems, or whether she perceives them differently.

You want to learn about how Johnny behaves when he is away from home, with other children and adults.

You expect to learn how the teacher perceives his behavior.

You expect to learn about the classroom that Johnny spends so much time in. If Johnny is having academic or behavioral problems, you expect to find out whether the academic and behavioral climate in that classroom might be aggravating his problems.

Most important, you want to learn as much about the teacher as you do about Johnny. Is her perception of Johnny positive and optimistic—or is it unfocused, biased, and wildly inaccurate? Does she care about Johnny's problems? Does she want to help him? Is she even *capable* of helping him? Or is she wasting Johnny's time—possibly a large proportion of his educational life?

To sum up, for parents, the most important reason for the parent-teacher conference is to gather information. For the incompetent or inadequate teacher, the most important reason for the parent-teacher conference is to obscure information—or at least to edit out any link between her expectations, standards, and methods and the student's travails.

Most parents prepare for the parent-teacher conference by composing a list—at least mentally—of what they wish to discuss with the teacher. That's a sound strategy, particularly if you have come to know the teacher as an ally in your child's education. But if you suspect that the teacher may be part of the problem, or if you simply do not know how skilled, sensitive, or professional your child's teacher really is, I suggest that rather than spend your time preparing for the unknown you invest your energies in listening—and listening carefully—to what the teacher says in the conference. The teacher's comments may reveal little you didn't already know about your child, but they will disclose a great deal about the teacher, his attitudes, his methods, and his prejudices. By asking the right questions, and listening carefully to the answers, you will be able to clarify and confirm what you have learned from your child. Most of all, you will be able to identify accurately the source of the problem and act on your child's behalf.

In the pages to come, we will meet some of the teachers at Water Street School and see what they say about some common academic and behavior problems, similar to the problems Johnny might be having. These vignettes, based on the most common problems that arise among schoolchildren, illustrate typical parent-teacher conversations. From them, you may learn what questions to ask in order to get information about your child. Perhaps more important, these vignettes may show you how to listen for the message behind the teacher's words.

2

Academic Concerns

In some ways, schools started out like factories. About a hundred years ago, we took children out of the factories and put them into factorylike schools. We had faith in the manufacturing industry's approach, thinking that it could improve education the way it had improved production in other industries. We thought of learning as the child's job, the school as her place of employment, and the teacher as her job foreman. Her manufactured product was a series of papers—homework, classwork, and tests—and the teacher served as the quality-control inspector.

Today, some schools still seem like factories, and some teachers still think like assembly line supervisors. They check the flow of the child's work as it comes down the assembly line, and if any product doesn't meet the standards, it gets tossed into the reject bin. If your child produces too many rejects, the teacher will call you for a conference.

While the skilled teacher views an academic problem as a perhaps difficult but certainly not insurmountable challenge, the bad teacher uses it as his ace in the hole. Because the problem can be quantified, the teacher can establish undeniably that there is a problem. Rather than address your questions or concerns, he can simply say, "Let's take a look at my grade book, and I'll show you how Julie is doing this semester." He can also let you know, seemingly authoritatively, that the fault is entirely your child's. "I'm sorry to say that the other children don't seem to have any trouble with this material," he'll report, as if daring you to come up with any evidence that your child might actually be a capable student.

And do you defend your child in the face of such incontrovertible evidence? Most parents don't. It's hard to argue with a stack of dismal papers or with a string of low grades. Anyone would have to acknowledge that there is a problem. But blaming your child for the problem might be jumping to the wrong conclusion.

The fundamental flaw is in the teacher's thinking. In truth, the school is not a factory, the child is not some factory drone, and the child's schoolwork is not the product. If there is any usefulness to a "manufacturing" analogy at all, then the product of the system is not the schoolwork; the product is the *child*. If quality is to be measured, then we must measure the child, not the schoolwork. Poor work, in itself, is not the problem, although it is definitely symptomatic of a problem. Even if your child is the only one having trouble, there are numerous other possible explanations for his difficulty.

Grades are not always what they seem. Ideally, a grade is a measure of the child's achievement on a specific body of academic work. But it's an imperfect measure for two reasons.

First, the grade is assigned by the teacher and is therefore subjective. Putting a grade on the quality of a child's original story is simply documenting an opinion. Compiling a report card grade from a series of assignments requires many subjective judgments about what's important and what's not. Even when a teacher gives grades on an objective basis, there are some underlying subjective choices. For example, when your child gets a C+, what does it mean? It could mean that her work is slightly above average compared to that of her classmates, slightly above average nationally for her grade, slightly above average for her age group, slightly above expectations for her reading group. Possibly the grade doesn't compare her to other students at all; maybe it means that she got 78 percent of the answers right, regardless of how well her classmates did. Which meaning has the teacher chosen?

Furthermore, teachers sometimes include nonacademic factors in the grades they assign. They might lower grades (usually for boys) if they don't like a child's classroom behavior. In some schools, teachers routinely take off points for spelling. A child who was born a poor speller, therefore, would have his grade in history, science, composition, and even math diminished every time he put pencil to paper. So you can't make assumptions about what a grade really means. It's not a measure of the child, and it may not even be an accurate measure of the child's work.

The second reason that grades are imperfect measures of the child is that they give no indication as to *why* the child is doing well or poorly. If Sally is getting a better grade than Johnny, it could be that Sally is smarter than Johnny, or that Sally works harder than Johnny and gets her assignments in on time. Maybe Sally is no better at understanding the work, but pays much better attention to detail. Or there may be another reason, one that Johnny has less control over. Maybe Johnny has a learning disability that should have been diagnosed by this teacher or a previous teacher. Maybe Johnny's mode of learning doesn't match up with the teacher's mode of teaching. If Sally absorbs information by listening and has a teacher who loves to lecture, Sally is nearly guaranteed a good grade—while Johnny, who is a tactile learner, is out of luck because the teacher doesn't provide the physical, "hands-on" materials he needs. Maybe Sally has a better memory, or had a better teacher the previous year. The bottom line is that Johnny's grades make him look like a failure; but that doesn't necessarily mean that he *is* a failure, that his difficulty is entirely his fault, or that the teacher is faultless.

It is crucial that, even in the face of hard evidence, a parent should withhold judgment until after conferring with the teacher. In the course of a conference, the teacher's thoughts and attitudes may reveal that she is creating or compounding Johnny's difficulties. But how can a parent get beyond the hard evidence of the grade book to find out what is really happening to Johnny and why? How can a parent get beyond the teacher's defense mechanisms to help Johnny? The anecdotes that follow are based on the academic problems most commonly discussed at parent-teacher conferences. You will probably find parts of each anecdote that represent your own child and your own dilemmas. These anecdotes will show you how to go beyond the teachers' words to hear what the teachers are really saying—about your child and about themselves.

Jill Doesn't Read Well

The first report card of the year has come in, and Jill has earned consistently good grades except for a low to middling grade in reading. The reading grade is something of a surprise to you, because you thought school was going pretty well for Jill. She seems enthusiastic about school and she loves her teacher, Miss Butler. Miss Butler doesn't appear to be any rocket scientist, but she really doesn't need the IQ of a rocket scientist to interest seven-year-olds in rockets or science. For a primary school teacher, there are qualities more important than IQ, and Miss Butler has them. She is patient, enthusiastic, compassionate, and has a comfortable lap.

You have looked in on Miss Butler's classroom and everything seemed fine. The children were busy and happy, and Miss Butler was generous with praise and positive reinforcement. Jill's papers have come home with lots of happy-face stickers and rubber-stamped words of encouragement. All that makes it surprising to find that Jill is struggling with her reading. You ask for a conference with Miss Butler, hoping that there has been some clerical error and that Jill is actually doing well.

WHAT'S GOING ON HERE?

Jill had a terrific teacher last year. The teacher sent home newsletters to keep parents aware of class activities. Jill's in-class and homework assignments always came home, complete with clear, specific written comments. You knew what was going on in the classroom.

This year you aren't getting the same communication from the teacher. You assume it's because Jill is a year

older and can be trusted to convey information from
school to home. You are sure everything's fine, especially
since Miss Butler is so nice. Then the report card arrives,
and you suddenly realize that everything is *not* okay. You
stop and think; have you seen *any* comments or messages
from Miss Butler this year? No, you haven't. Only stickers
and stamps. You don't really know what her handwriting
looks like, or even if she knows how to write. . . .

You talk to some of the other parents, and they tell the
same story. They have not seen any written communication from the teacher either. And Jill's situation may be
worse than you feared; it turns out that in America's second grade classrooms, almost all the children get very
high marks on their report cards. Even the children at the
very bottom of the class are given average marks. So Jill's
low to middling grade could be the worst in the class.

And you don't know why. You have seen the hodge-
podge of papers that have come home, and they haven't
given you a clear picture of what's happening in the reading class. Is Jill being taught to read, or is she just being
tested on her reading ability? If she has a learning problem, is the teacher aware of it? Does the teacher have the
knowledge and skill to find a learning problem if there is
one?

Jill may have a reading problem, but that might not
be the only problem. Maybe the teacher is the core of the
problem because she inflates grades, can't diagnose, can't
teach well, or can't read well herself (see Chapter 6).

WHAT TO ASK THE TEACHER

If Jill is a poor reader, she is confronting the most serious problem an elementary school student can face in

school. Reading is not just a subject on the report card; it is the key to every other subject she will encounter in school. In a real sense, reading is the teacher itself, more of a teacher than the person who stands at the front of the classroom. If Jill is a weak reader, it is critical to find out why and to do something about it immediately. And you will need the teacher's observations and insight to find the causes.

The root of Jill's reading problem can be very complex, because reading is a complex issue. The causes of Jill's poor reading might be poor eyesight, poor visual perception, poor phonetic skills, poor memory, or poor teaching. A good teacher should have given her the appropriate skills, and should be familiar with the huge range of physical, psychological, and educational problems that could contribute to poor reading skills.

The word *reading* carries a lot of baggage; it means different things to different people. It also means different things for children of different ages. Some schools have elaborate reading programs that define reading as thousands of sequential steps. In my opinion, their programs are rarely very effective. It is more useful to define reading in general terms. At any grade level, reading means understanding the printed symbol. In kindergarten, reading means *understanding the letter*— comprehending that the symbol A, B, or C stands for a particular sound. Once that skill has been mastered, reading means *understanding the word*—knowing that it stands for a particular object, action, idea, and so on. When the student can read words fluently, then reading is *understanding the sentence.* Later, reading means *understanding the paragraph*—finding and comprehending the main idea.

If reading means understanding, then a teacher should test reading ability by testing understanding. But most teachers don't do that; they test reading by testing pronunciation, vocabulary, memory, or intelligence. All of these things are related to reading, but they are not the same as reading.

To get a true picture of Jill's reading skills, you will have to pin Miss Butler down with some specific questions:

- How is Jill at sounding out new words?
- Can Jill break words down into syllables?
- How is her pronunciation?
- How is her speed?
- How is her vocabulary?
- How is her comprehension?
- When is her reading weakest—during what time of day, doing which subjects, with which groups of children?
- What is the report card grade based on? Tests, oral reading, speed, vocabulary, comprehension, or some combination of these and other factors?
- If the grade is based on tests, what tests were used? Do they really measure reading skills rather than memory, intelligence, listening, or pronunciation?
- Does the report card grade compare her to other students, or does it reflect her test and homework scores? If the latter, how *does* Jill compare to the other students?
- Is there a specific reading class? How long is it? How large is Jill's reading group? What fraction of the teacher's time is spent with Jill's group? What amount of time?

- What training has the teacher had in teaching reading?
- What reading method is used in this class? (Does the teacher have a coherent answer to this question?)
- Where is the classroom library? Are there regularly scheduled visits to the school library? To the public library?
- Does the teacher read to the children?

READING SKILLS: WHAT THE TEACHER IS LIKELY TO SAY . . . AND WHAT IT COULD MEAN

Asking the right questions during the parent-teacher conference is a great way to begin the information-gathering process, but in order to get the clearest possible picture of your child's classroom situation, it is crucial that you also learn to interpret the teacher's answers and comments.

Here are a few examples of the possible meanings or issues behind the teachers' statements about your child's reading skills.

MISS JOHNSON: Joe has trouble sounding out new words.

POSSIBLE MEANING: Joe has never been taught phonics, the process of associating sounds with letters. The best readers have always taught themselves, often before they started school. Educators have observed that these top performers read by sight (without noticeably sounding out each letter), so they think all students should learn to read by sight. This used to be called "see and say"; now it is called "whole language." By any name, it doesn't work.

You can't draw general principles from a small sample at the top end of the range of abilities. Children who are not at the very top of the range don't learn to read by seeing, and if they aren't taught phonics, they have no way to learn to read at all.

MR. THOMAS: Mindy doesn't read out loud very well.

POSSIBLE MEANING: Mindy has had very little practice at reading. Do the math yourself: Reading class lasts forty minutes, and there are three reading groups of eight children each. Mr. Thomas listens to Mindy read *about two minutes per day.* Mindy reads to other members of the reading group about four minutes per day, for a total of six minutes per day.

ANOTHER POSSIBLE MEANING: It is possible for a child to pronounce sentences beautifully without understanding much; this is a poor reader, no matter how good he sounds. On the other hand, it is possible for a child to understand well, even though he pronounces poorly. This child also has a problem, but it is not really a reading problem and should be handled differently than a reading problem. It could be a hearing problem or a visual problem.

MISS TRENT: Stanley's grade is based on . . . let me look in my grade book.

POSSIBLE MEANING: Miss Trent has a slot on the report card for reading, and a bunch of canned tests that were provided by the company that published the reading text. All year long, she just follows the dots. Consequently, she doesn't really know much about Stanley's reading skills. She probably couldn't give you separate responses about his speed, vocabulary, and comprehension; all she has is a vague overall impression about his reading ability. She can't diagnose specific learning problems and she can't give you the information you will need to help Stanley.

MRS. WILSON: Dawn doesn't remember what she reads.

POSSIBLE MEANING: If she doesn't remember what she has read silently, she may in fact have a comprehension problem. But if she has problems only with material she has read orally in class, the problem may be something else. She may have performance anxiety. She may be concentrating so hard on proper pronunciation that she isn't thinking about the meaning.

MR. GRANT: Mitchell reverses letters and words when he reads.

POSSIBLE MEANING: Depending on Mitchell's age, this could be important or trivial. Reversing letters is common for beginning readers, who are just learning that writing goes from left to right. After all, there is nothing instinctive about reading left to right; Hebrew goes from right to left, Chinese goes from top to bottom, and some ancient languages went *boustrophedon,* "as the ox turns," back and forth across the page.

If reversals are plentiful, or if they persist beyond the age of eight, they may be evidence of a visual perception

problem. But a young reader's occasional reversals
should not be a cause for alarm.

MR. GRANT: Alyssa has dyslexia.

POSSIBLE MEANING: There are dozens of possible meanings. This
book avoids the use of the word *dyslexia* because it is an
umbrella term that points neither to a specific condition
nor to a specific remedy. It is variously defined and variously understood; the translation is simply, "can't read."
The different conditions subsumed under *dyslexia* are discussed briefly in this book. If a teacher uses the word, ask
him exactly what he means by it.

MISS HENDERSON: We have parents and aides who read to the
children.

POSSIBLE MEANING: Miss Henderson doesn't do the reading herself because she doesn't read very well. She has about an
eighth grade reading ability.

MR. CLARK: I have a teaching credential from Mirrortest College.

POSSIBLE MEANING: The truth is that there are thousands of colleges in this country, and only forty of them are truly "selective," meaning that they accept less than half of their
applicants. Of the others, the overwhelming majority
have no entrance standards at all. Mr. Clark went to a
college that accepts anyone whose reflection appears in

a mirror, and got through with a combination of a good memory and good friends. He was given good advice by the career counselor, who told him, "If you're a dumb jock, major in physical education. If you're just dumb, major in education." *Possible importance of the teaching credential to your child:* None.

WHAT TO DO

You may find, in the course of the conference, that Jill's reading skills really are below those of the other students. Check to see whether those other students had other, better teachers in the previous grade, and thus started the year ahead of Jill. If Jill's background is equal to her peers' yet her skills are lower, and her teacher can't give you any reasons why, then you need to establish the presence or absence of a learning problem. Ask the teacher to arrange an evaluation of Jill's reading skills by an expert.

Most schools or school districts have a reading specialist, a special-education teacher, or another teacher experienced in diagnosing reading problems. Those jobs exist for the purpose of helping the struggling students, which also helps the teachers of the struggling students. Therefore, your child's teacher will not be offended if you request such services, particularly if you phrase your request carefully. You don't say, "I don't trust your judgment. Get me an expert." Instead you say, "Jill's scores are low. Can the schools help *us* to find the best way to improve Jill's reading?"

You may suspect, after the conference, that part of Jill's reading problem is poor teaching, or that her teacher is semiliterate. What can you do? Later chapters of this book will help you transfer Jill to a better classroom if need be, but before you take that step, there are two things you can do.

1. Encourage the teacher to schedule activities that are tailored to Jill's needs. You want her to get more time and personal attention from the classroom teacher or from the reading specialist. If the classroom has a teacher's aide, that aide will probably be less skilled and less experienced than the regular teacher, so you don't want Jill sloughed off onto the aide. On the other hand, if the head teacher is a poor teacher, and if the aide will give Jill individual attention, then perhaps Jill will be better off with the aide.

2. More important is that you will have to work with Jill at home. If the schools aren't teaching Jill to read, you will have to do it yourself. Where will you find the time? It won't be hard. The amount of time Jill spends interacting directly with the teacher is probably less than six minutes per day. Listen to her read for only twenty minutes a day, and you've already given her more reading time and attention than she gets in a week at school. Ask her to read for you; then, at the end of each paragraph, ask her to recap what the paragraph said.

There is no substitute for pure volume of reading; it builds vocabulary, it builds speed, and it builds comprehension. Children who don't read will be as bad off as children who can't read. To give your child enough time to read in volume, enforce this rule: She should spend at least as much time reading books (over and beyond school assignments) as she spends watching TV and playing video games.

HOW LONG TO WAIT BEFORE EXPECTING RESULTS

Reading problems are not amenable to a "quick fix." You should not expect any improvement in the short term (under a month), even if your child has a specific learning problem that is identified immediately. But reading skills are affected by "time on task"; if your child starts immediately to spend more time reading, her skills will improve over time.

If your child's problem is a bad teacher, you will have a very long wait before you can expect results from the school's actions. Her teacher will still be bad, long after your child has passed on to another class. You will need to assess the seriousness of the problem, and then decide whether to stagger through the remainder of the year in the bad teacher's class, provide your child with at-home help or a tutor, or actively try to get her out of that bad teacher's classroom as soon as possible.

Jeffrey Doesn't Do His Assigned Work

Ms. Sauer welcomes you to her classroom, where all the desks are in parallel rows like lines of chicks streaming behind the mother-hen desk at the front of the room. Everything is tidy, from her pristine desktop to the optimistic homilies that adorn her bulletin boards. On the wall, you note her "Water Street School Teacher of the Year" award. It dates from twenty years ago.

As the conference begins, she announces the reason for the conference: Jeffrey isn't getting his work done. Ms. Sauer shows you her grade book, and sure enough, next to Jeffrey's name are numerous incompletes. Ms.

Sauer is disappointed at Jeffrey's failure to meet his responsibilities, and her tone does not mask her disapproval of his laziness or other character flaws.

Her comments are a surprise to you. You have never known Jeffrey to be lazy. If anything, his problem might be *too much* energy. Nor are you aware of any missing assignments. You have checked his homework every night since school began in September.

WHAT'S GOING ON HERE?

You look again at the grade book, and the evidence there is plain. Ms. Sauer has a record of every single assignment since the beginning of school, and the marks that follow Jeffrey's name are sporadic. And there is no questioning Ms. Sauer's grade book. Her record keeping, like her classroom, is meticulous. As you try to erase the words *obsessive compulsive* from your mind, you give her credit for trying to be accurate and fair.

Jeffrey's failure to complete these assignments could be laziness, although you doubt that. It could also be Jeffrey's protest that all these trivial assignments are just busywork, or that he doesn't like being treated like a number. It could mean that he is a perfectionist, that he didn't get the assignment, or is careless or confused. It could be a strategy he uses to avoid failure. You can see the blank spaces in the grade book, but you won't know what they are saying about Jeffrey until the teacher tells you more.

WHAT TO ASK THE TEACHER

If your child has accumulated a mountain of incomplete work, begin by focusing specifically on the kinds of assignments the child doesn't do. Were they classwork or homework? If classwork, which subjects? Were they turned in unfinished, or not turned in at all? What is the quality of the work your child *has* done? Is the teacher sure your child understood what was assigned? More important, did the teacher explain how to do the assignment? Was the assignment busywork, or did it contribute to some worthwhile objective?

WHAT THE TEACHER IS LIKELY TO SAY . . . AND WHAT IT COULD MEAN

Once again, the key to interpreting a struggling child's behavior may lie in interpreting the teacher's answers and comments. These examples may help clarify any hidden clues to your child's difficulties.

MS. BOYD: Allen works too slowly.

POSSIBLE MEANING: Allen is a perfectionist. Why does Ms. Boyd have a problem with this? Maybe she doesn't give the students enough time to finish a job properly.

ANOTHER POSSIBLE MEANING: Allen lacks confidence that he is doing his work correctly. A sympathetic teacher could solve this problem with lots of encouragement and positive reinforcement. A bad teacher can make this problem a whole lot worse simply by being insensitive to the problem. Incomplete assignments do create record-keeping inconveniences that are galling to people like Ms. Boyd. But if neat records are more important than Allen's needs, then the problem does not lie with Allen.

MR. GREGORY: Nicole doesn't follow directions.

POSSIBLE MEANING: Nicole doesn't listen well. Maybe she has a hearing problem or an auditory perception problem.

ANOTHER POSSIBLE MEANING: Nicole doesn't listen well because her neighbors are rowdy or too sociable.

YET ANOTHER POSSIBLE MEANING: Nicole listens well, but the assignment wasn't explained well. The explanation of how to do the work may have been given to the teacher's satisfaction, but not to the students' satisfaction. Maybe Nicole is like all the others: too embarrassed to admit that she didn't understand. Poor Nicole may be in a panic, afraid to get a zero for a missing assignment, but without a clue about what to do.

MS. FRANKLIN: Often, Kurt almost finishes the work.

POSSIBLE MEANING: He doesn't want to finish, because experience has taught him that finishing an assignment is always followed by Judgment Time. Someone will take his work and make a judgment, usually negative, about the quality of the work. This judgment may also include some "constructive criticism" of the quality of his work habits, beliefs, attitude, hearing, and may degenerate into a global criticism of everything about the child. Or the overly sensitive child may take any constructive criticism as a searingly personal insult. One way to postpone Judgment Time is to postpone finishing the work, so Kurt has developed a tendency to leave his tasks unfinished.

MR. MARTINEZ: Tricia forgets assignments.

POSSIBLE MEANING: Tricia does a poor job of writing down assignments in her book, and her memory is not trustworthy.

ANOTHER POSSIBLE MEANING: She carefully writes down the assignments, but often loses the paper she wrote them on. Or she remembers the paper but forgets the necessary textbooks. Or she does the assignment and forgets where she put it, or she forgets to bring it to school. This sort of thing often happens to perfectly normal boys and girls with chronically untied shoelaces.

YET ANOTHER POSSIBLE MEANING: Some teachers give out the homework assignments in a haphazard manner, making it hard to record and remember them. Most teachers reserve a particular part of the blackboard for homework assignments, and they reserve the last few minutes of the school day to make sure the assignments are written down. For long-term assignments, students should get frequent reminders of due dates. But not all teachers are so well organized.

MS. DANNER: Michael doesn't even try to finish his work.

POSSIBLE MEANING: Michael has tried different ways to please this teacher and he can't find a way to make her satisfied. Her standards are so vague, or so arbitrary, or keep rising beyond whatever Michael does, that he has just given up.

WHAT TO DO

Your child isn't getting all the required work done, and the teacher seems obsessed with getting his grade book filled. Don't buy into the teacher's obsession. Agree that there is a problem here, but the holes in the grade book are only the symptom, not the problem itself. What you must do is focus on your child and help him become a successful student.

First, you need to determine whether your son or daughter is being held back by a learning problem that has not yet been diagnosed or remedied. Some expert diagnostic testing may be called for here.

Second, you and the teacher need to help the child get organized. Begin by tidying the desks at home and school, and organizing all notebooks, cubbyholes, and lockers. Chaos manifests itself in various ways, in the desk and in the mind. Then provide your young scholar with an assignment book, or a particular place in a notebook for assignments. With the teacher, arrange a system that enables both of you to check his assignment sheet daily— the teacher to make sure the assignments have been recorded (and the textbooks needed to complete them), and you to make sure the work has been satisfactorily completed (including finishing any incomplete classwork).

Look around the classroom. Does it appear that the assignments are posted in an obvious place and are easily visible from your child's seat? Ask the teacher whether he has explained how to do the assignments, and how he checks to make sure his students do, indeed, understand. In the lower grades especially, find out if his explanations include hands-on practice, or if it is only verbal instruction.

Third, take the emotional pulse of the classroom. Volunteer as a classroom helper or assistant. Then try to sense how the teacher interacts with the children in gen-

eral, and with your child in particular. Compare what she
says about your child to what your child says about her.
Does she really know who your son or daughter is, aside
from those entries in her grade book?

Fourth, find out where your child sits during different
activities in the course of the day, and which students sit
near her. This is especially important if her work is missing only in certain subjects. Can she see and hear instructions from her seat? Ask the teacher where he does most
of the instruction—at the board, in his seat? Does he
move around among the students? Does he instruct individuals, groups, or the class as a whole?

Finally, you can help your child with his homework.
Occasionally, you may run into an arrogant teacher who
tells you not to help your child. No teacher should claim
to be the only fount of knowledge in a bone-dry desert.
There is very little magic in a teaching credential, and
any intelligent parent can be the child's best teacher.
Schoolteachers mean well, but their intentions often exceed their capabilities.

Of course, this doesn't mean that you should do your
second-grader's work for her. But you can make sure that
your struggling student understands the assignment and
knows *how* to go about doing it. If your child is less than
eleven years old, you can also check the work after it is
done. At about that age, children rightly begin to assert
some independence from their parents; checking an ado-
lescent's work may make her feel that you are "standing
in judgment" of her, and that could lead to power conflicts that poison your whole relationship. So you may not
wish to check a preteenager's completed work, because
the price may be too high. Your child will let you know

when he or she is too old to have homework closely supervised.

HOW LONG BEFORE YOU CAN EXPECT RESULTS

If your child's problem is simply lack of organization, you can expect results immediately. As soon as he or she is provided with a system of recording assignments, and knows that you and the teacher will be communicating via the assignment sheet, the work will get done. At that point, it is crucial that neither you nor the teacher let up on your demands and allow the child to slip back into the old disorganized pattern. Continue to monitor the student's progress closely for several months, still supervising but gradually making your supervision less obvious. In that time, you hope, your child will develop the habit of recording and fulfilling assignments.

If, for example, your daughter isn't getting the work done because she is too sociable in class, that is another problem that can be solved quickly. As soon as the teacher is aware of the problem, she can rearrange the seating or the class grouping to remove her from temptation. A good teacher will also find other ways to reward her for focusing more on the work than on the social aspects of class.

If, on the other hand, your son is unable to do the work because of a learning problem, then it may take longer to solve the problem. Clearly, the situation won't improve unless the problem is correctly diagnosed and until remediation has been prescribed. Some problems, for example nearsightedness, can be remedied quickly. Other problems may be more serious and may require months or years of attention. As a general rule, you can begin to expect results soon after an accurate diagnosis, even before any remedial activity starts. Often the child is so relieved that he's no longer being blamed, his attitude and his work improve immediately.

If the root of the problem lies with the teacher, you should not expect positive results in the foreseeable future. Nothing you can do is likely to change the teacher, and there is no chance the teacher will spontaneously improve. All you can do is to provide your child with the teaching and the structure that *should have been* provided by the teacher, and do what you can to get through the year. If the teacher's problem is more serious, or if it creates more serious problems for your son or daughter, then you will have to take more extreme measures. Later chapters in this book will advise you on that.

Alison Is Capable of Better Work

Mrs. Caffrey says that Alison is capable of better work, and she is right. Alison probably is capable of better work. None of us works at 100 percent of our ability 100 percent of the time. Mrs. Caffrey points out that although Alison does all her assignments, she doesn't do them as well as she could. She thinks Alison could do better.

WHAT'S GOING ON HERE?

It's nice to know that Mrs. Caffrey has a high opinion of Alison's ability. You share her feeling that Alison has the ability to do excellent work. And her comments confirm a nagging feeling you have had, that Alison hasn't been doing her best.

She does her homework, and you check to make sure it was done. Sometimes she does the work quickly and effortlessly. Sometimes she sits at her desk and takes forever to finish. Sometimes she tells you that she did it in school, or that she can finish it tomorrow in school. When she has a test, she studies for it, sometimes for hours. But even when she puts in the long hours, the results are never outstanding. Her test scores are adequate but not impressive, never low enough to worry Alison and never high enough to make you excited. Her report card grades, like her test scores, are somewhere in the middle. In fact, her grades are so unremarkable that Mrs. Caffrey would never call for a parent-teacher conference; you are only having one because *you* asked for it, or because district policy requires them.

Alison's lack of enthusiasm is mirrored by Mrs. Caffrey's. She has been at Water Street School for a long time, and you wonder if she is teaching on autopilot. Her classroom is orderly but unexciting, and nothing there seems to have piqued Alison's imagination. When Alison brings home an exciting narrative of something that happened at school, it's always about the playground or the lunchroom, never the classroom; and it's never about anything she's learning.

WHAT TO ASK THE TEACHER

You and the teacher agree that Alison is a girl with more potential than she is showing, and you want to know why she is not doing better work. There are numerous questions you want to ask the teacher, including many of the same questions you would ask if Alison were not doing the work at all. For example, you want to know whether Alison's poorest work is in a particular subject; on homework rather than classwork or tests; or on things she should have memorized. Does she do better with things heard in class, or with things read in the textbook? What kinds of questions can she best answer: fact questions, inference questions, fill-in-the-blanks questions, or essay questions?

You might ask Mrs. Caffrey for her opinion about why Alison's work is so mediocre. Does she think she is lacking in motivation, or study skills, or brainpower? Can she back up her opinion with facts and observations?

WHAT THE TEACHER IS LIKELY TO SAY . . .
AND WHAT IT COULD MEAN

It can be difficult to tell who needs to focus more on classwork, the teacher or the student. But teacher comments like these can give you a clue as to who needs to try a little harder in the classroom.

MRS. CAFFREY: I give them a test at the end of each chapter. I do not give them study sheets.

POSSIBLE MEANING: Alison has no idea what to study for a test, and the teacher gives her no clues.

Mrs. Caffrey has a great advantage over Alison and the other children in that she already knows the material being taught. She already has the "big picture," the overall understanding of the course and what its objectives are. She has been through the course once or twice or thirteen times, and she knows how the course objectives relate to each other.

If Mrs. Caffrey were a good teacher, she would have carefully explained to the children what the course is all about. She would have given them an overview of the skills and abilities they would work on during the term, and would have given them a summary of the facts they would learn. At the beginning of each new chapter, Mrs. Caffrey would have again previewed the course's requirements and goals, so the children would know where their educational journey is headed.

In a good class with a good teacher, the classes will lead the children toward their announced objectives. The children will be better travelers along the path to learning because they know where they are going, and they know what they have to do to get there.

At the end of the chapter, there is usually a test. In a good class with a good teacher, the children know what to study for the test. They have known all along, because each test has been a fair measure of the chapter's goals, and the students have known all along what the goals of the chapter are. They know what to study and how to study. But Alison's teacher never outlined the goals, either before the chapter or at the end. Consequently, Alison can't tell headline from footnote, what's important to study, and what is tangential to the course's goals.

MRS. CAFFREY: Alison needs to study harder for tests.
POSSIBLE MEANING: Mrs. Caffrey has never taught study skills, so Alison has no idea how to study for a test.

Unfortunately for most children, a chapter in a textbook is simply a long string of unrelated assignments, containing an infinitely long string of unrelated facts. There may exist, somewhere in space, a set of goals that tie everything together and make it easier to understand, but too often, the goals are not made plain to the children, or they are explained later, or explained in words the children don't understand. The result is that a class that seems well organized and coherent to the teacher, may not seem at all organized to the child. The child may be so overwhelmed by the avalanche of facts that she doesn't see the unifying concepts that would help her understand how the facts work together. It is the teacher's job to make sure that the child sees this "big picture."

A child can remember fifty facts for a history test, but only if she understands the "big picture." If she can mentally organize the chapter into headings and subheadings, she can place four facts here, three facts there, and easily memorize them all because each heading and subheading has only a few items. Without the "big picture," the child can't possibly learn a list of fifty random facts that are, to her, unrelated.

Children need to be taught to study "from the top down," learning the overall concepts first, then the subconcepts, then related facts. Left to their devices, children will study "from the bottom up," trying to learn the separate facts without organizing them into concepts. If Mrs. Caffrey hasn't taught Alison the right way to study, she is likely to make comments like "Alison does poorly on essay questions." This might mean that Alison doesn't know which ones in that avalanche of facts are related to the essay question. And she's never been taught how to organize facts into an essay structure.

Or Mrs. Caffrey might say, "Alison does poorly on fill-in-the-blanks questions." That wouldn't be surprising, because nobody can memorize fifty unrelated facts, and no intelligent teacher would ask them to. What is being measured by this kind of test—the child's understanding, or the child's memory skills? If Alison gets 78 percent right, does she get a C+ in history or a C+ in memory?

MRS. CAFFREY: Alison needs to work harder on her homework.
POSSIBLE MEANING: Alison can tell you what the assignment is, but she doesn't really understand what the teacher wants and expects.

Most children start with a built-in desire to do well and a built-in desire to please the teacher. It is quite rare to find a truly lazy child. (It's easy to find a child addicted to TV or video games, but that's another story.) Most children think they are studying as hard as they can, and it's true that they are studying as hard as they know how. The problem is that they don't know how to study because nobody has ever taught them how.

Find out from Mrs. Caffrey what she has done to teach study skills. Is there a specific study skills unit, and is it taught early in the year? More important, does the teacher teach study skills throughout the year? For each different type of assignment, she should have explained how to do it and what standard of performance she expects. Alison knows what to do if the assignment is "Do page 37, problems 1 through 10, answer true or false." But she needs more help and guidance if the assignment is to write an essay on chipmunks. Alison may not have been taught how to do research, make notes, or organize an essay.

In any class where study skills have not been emphasized, there is a breakdown in communication every time
homework is assigned. For example, let's look at a typical
homework assignment: "Read pages 235 to 239." To Alison, this assignment means, "Run your eyes across each
word on pages 235 to 239, then close the book." To Mrs.
Caffrey, the assignment actually means, "On pages 235 to
239, pick out the main idea and important facts from each
paragraph, then relate the main ideas to each other, so
that you comprehend the whole and its parts." It doesn't
even occur to Alison that the teacher expects all that,
when all Mrs. Caffrey has instructed her to do is "Read."
She has never explained it to Alison. So Alison goes right
along, doing badly in that subject and never figuring out
why.

Moreover, any assignment that directs children to
"Read pages 42 to 45 and answer questions 1 to 5" almost
encourages them to use poor study skills. Knowing that
the only part of the assignment that will be collected and
graded is the "questions 1 to 5" part, the students focus
their time and attention on that part of the assignment.
Unfortunately, the important part of the assignment is
the "Read pages 42 to 45" part, but that part will not be
collected or graded, so Alison skimps on that part. The
end result: A paper is turned in for each assignment, but
it's not a very good paper because it represents a poor
understanding of the content. And at the end of each
chapter, Alison's test is mediocre; she's done all the work
that Mrs. Caffrey asked for, but she never knew what
Mrs. Caffrey really wanted.

∞

MRS. CAFFREY: Alison doesn't seem to care about her work.

POSSIBLE MEANING: Alison is just as excited about the work as Mrs. Caffrey is. As the poster says, a child learns what she lives, and Alison is taking her cue from her teacher. Mrs. Caffrey has no enthusiasm for the work, so why should Alison?

WHAT TO DO

Alison is getting the work done, but isn't doing it very well. You and the teacher both know that Alison could do better, but you aren't sure why she isn't working up to par or what to do about it.

In the parent-teacher conference, you need to ask Mrs. Caffrey some questions about her goals. Does she have goals for the year, for the course, or even for the chapter? Then ask whether Alison is aware of these goals, and whether the goals have been explained to her in a way she could understand. And find out whether the class that is being taught has any relationship to the goals that have been announced.

You know you are in trouble if you ask Mrs. Caffrey about her goals, and she says that her goal is to get through the textbook. The trouble is even worse if she has abandoned hope of getting through the textbook and her only goal is to follow the textbook as far as she can. In either case, she has no goals at all.

In addition to finding out about goals, you need to ask Mrs. Caffrey about her standards and expectations. Has she stated her expectations to Alison often enough and clearly enough for her to understand what she needs to do? It is not constructive for a teacher to tell Alison to work harder without teaching her *how* to work harder.

Putting in longer hours will probably not solve Alison's problem. She needs to learn how to use her hours more efficiently.

Also at the conference, look around the room for signs of life. Are the bulletin board displays shopworn from years of reuse? Do you see any student projects, any activities that require ingenuity and enthusiasm? Does the teacher discourage spontaneity and creativity? (Have you ever seen an art exhibit of thirty-four children's versions of the same sunflower?)

At home, there are various things you can do to help Alison. Your most important contribution would be to help her with study habits. Each child must learn that the written part of homework is the least important part, because *understanding* is the most important part. You could help Alison identify the fundamental concepts of each chapter, so she can organize her mental picture and study from the top down. The main points are often summarized at the beginning or end of the chapter, or can be identified by looking at the chapter subheadings.

If the teacher has no enthusiasm for a topic, and Alison has none either, you can't pretend that the topic is fascinating and that Alison should be captivated by it. That would be insulting Alison, insinuating that she is incapable of appreciating the fine qualities of the topic. What you *can* do is show Alison the joy of being competent, the feeling that "I can do this. I can master this topic. I am controlling it; it is not controlling me."

HOW LONG BEFORE YOU CAN EXPECT RESULTS

If you can convince Mrs. Caffrey to teach a unit on study skills, you could begin to see results immediately.

Even better, if she were to teach study skills within each unit, you would see immediate results. But don't hold your breath, waiting for a teacher to change her habits of a lifetime.

You can expect results only after *you* have taken on the responsibility of teaching study skills to Alison. And even then the results may not be immediate. You are trying to change Alison from a trained seal, motivated to capture and regurgitate facts on cue for the approval of someone else, into someone who learns because she likes to understand things and to feel competent.

An academic problem does not exist in a vacuum. If a child has academic problems, it will affect her emotional well-being and her behavior. Helping your child to understand her school subjects will help her feel good about herself.

And it works both ways; behavioral conflicts with the teacher will affect the child's academic performance in a negative way. A teacher who is insensitive, bullying, or confrontational will get less effort and less achievement from her students. In the next chapter, we will look at ways that bad teaching and learning disabilities can masquerade as behavior problems in children.

3

Behavioral Concerns

Scott scores! The crowd goes wild! He scores again!

Scoring in academics is a lot like scoring in the Olympics: The reward is always given to those who get higher scores on the test, do the work faster, go further in the book. Everything can be measured either by the higher, faster, further academic yardstick or the stopwatch, and more is always better. To win the prize, you have to be the leader of the pack, the top of the heap, the standard setter by whose achievement everyone else's progress is measured: highest, fastest, or furthest.

Rating a child's *behavior* requires a completely different perspective. Behavior is measured not on a yardstick with an ever-ascending scale but on a continuum that has two ends, such as these that appear below:

├────┼────┼────┼────┼────┼────┼────┤

SOCIAL ADJUSTMENT

├────┼────┼────┼────┼────┼────┼────┤

LOCUS OF CONTROL

It is clear to see why more is not better on such scales. For every imaginable behavioral trait—even positive traits like sensitivity, cooperation, or responsibility—being at either extreme end of the scale indicates a lack of balance. On the social adjustment scale, for example, you don't want Johnny to be hostile, but you also don't want him to be servile. On the locus of control scale (the child's perception of what controls his life—himself or outside forces?), you don't want Beth to be either egocentric or completely dependent. On any behavioral scale, the best place to be is in the middle, far from the misfits at each end.

Quantifying behavior is difficult and inexact. For any given behavior, experts may not agree on what constitutes the middle of the scale, or where the optimum point on the scale might be. On the citizenship scale, a child who questions authority might be rated high by his parents but low by his teacher (or vice versa, depending on whose authority has been questioned). On any scale, children will spread out along the entire continuum from Goody Two-shoes to the Demon Seed, with most of them somewhere in the middle. It is important to remember, however, that the middle includes a very wide range of behavior that is normal, and also includes almost as wide a range of behavior that is only "acceptable."

For many teachers, the range of "acceptable" behaviors is heavily skewed toward the Goody Two-shoes end of the continuum. An inflexible teacher may see no problem with training children to be mindless little conformists. For the teacher, there is a wide range of normal behavior that falls outside his range of acceptable behavior; and it is in that gray area that he comes into conflict with your child and with you.

Most children love to play, love to talk, sometimes

share and sometimes don't, fight for fairness and fight for fun. Some of these typical behaviors are normal for the playground but not acceptable for the classroom. Children know, or learn very quickly, what behavior is appropriate for each situation, although some children learn faster than others. Some children like to test the boundaries of acceptable behavior; they rattle the cage to see if the bars are loose. But if the cage is firm, they learn to live happily within the bars. Children have a natural desire to please their parents and teachers, and to live in harmony with their classmates. So most children will live within whatever set of rules are imposed.

But apparently not Davey.

The teacher has sent you a cryptic note stating that Davey is disrupting the class by talking too much. There is no further explanation about when he talks, to whom he talks, what he says when he talks, or how much is "too much."

Since it is likely that Davey's teacher may not share your view of what constitutes normal or even acceptable behavior, it will be up to you to decide whether Davey's behavior is 1) outside the wide range of normal behavior, or 2) normal but outside the range of appropriate classroom behavior, or 3) normal but outside *this teacher's* narrow range of acceptable behavior. The first option calls for therapy, the second calls for a corrective interview with Davey, and the third option leads countless parents into conflict with a teacher each and every school year.

Parents rely on teachers to provide them with honest, unprejudiced input on their children's behavior. Teachers—and particularly teachers' unions—suggest that because teachers are so highly trained and "professional," they are the most credible source possible for such information. So why would a teacher, one who has presumably dedicated her life to helping children, consider normal children's behavior to be a problem? There are several reasons.

The best reason is that more learning takes place in an orderly classroom. One child may learn more when he is enthusiastic or even boisterous, but the children around him may learn less because of the disruption. The optimum learning situation for all children may require that each child be less rowdy than normal. A good teacher will channel the normal enthusiastic behavior into acceptable activities; the bad teacher will simply forbid enthusiasm.

One of the worst reasons some teachers want to psychologically sedate their classes is just to make their jobs easier. Teaching is an exhausting job even under the best circumstances. The teacher is "onstage" all day long, juggling five balls at all times without losing her smile, maintaining thirty individual relationships simultaneously. Sometimes a lively child is the straw that breaks the camel's back, just slightly more than the teacher can cope with. As a parent, you know that badgered, beleaguered feeling; it overcomes all of us occasionally. On the other hand, some teachers want quiet classes all the time, just so they can maintain their serenity, stay in their chairs, and allow the class to teach itself.

Some teachers are heavy-handed in maintaining discipline because they have an ego problem. They may have gone into teaching because they like the feeling of control, and they can't control anyone over four feet tall. Teaching small children fulfills their need for power.

Other teachers have a superego problem. They have a heightened sense of "the way things are supposed to be."

In their minds, there are standards of behavior that must be met, and the children must be indoctrinated in the need to meet these rigorous and well-defined rules. Who knows what awful things may happen if these standards are not maintained in the classroom? Civilization may crumble, the empire may disintegrate, and anarchy may be loosed upon the world.

There are also some practical reasons that teachers attend first to the squeakiest wheel. In a class of thirty wild children, a teacher will consult first with the parents of the wildest child. In a quiet class of sixteen angels, some teachers will still try to get rid of the least angelic. In a statistical sense, it's easier to raise the average by eliminating the lowest child than by teaching more effectively to all the children.

Eliminating the rowdiest child also has another benefit to the teacher. Teachers are rewarded not for their students' achievement, but for the children's good behavior! Neither the principal nor the other teachers really know whether Mr. Tompkins is good at helping kids learn, but they all know whether he exhibits good classroom control and can make the kids march in straight lines. So any teacher who wants tenure, good evaluation ratings, and peer respect had better give behavior a higher priority than academics.

So there are a number of reasons, some very good ones, why you should question the teacher's desire to restrict what may be perfectly normal childhood behavior. But while you are at it, you should also ask yourself this: What has compelled the teacher to involve you in the discussion? What does she have to gain by calling a parent-teacher conference about Davey's behavior?

If Davey's behavior really is outside the normal range,

of course the parents should be notified so they can act in Davey's best interest. Similarly, if Davey's behavior is normal but unacceptable for the classroom, the parents should be included in the effort to retrain Davey. Any sincerely concerned educator knows that parents have information she will find useful in dealing effectively with Davey. At the very least, Davey's parents will know which approaches have succeeded with him in the past, and which have failed.

But if Davey's behavior is reasonable, and the teacher still finds it offensive, the teacher may have some ulterior motive in calling for a conference. It may be that, in the past, children have complained about the teacher's strictness or unfairness, and he wants to put his side of the story on the record. Perhaps he wants to defend his definition of "acceptable" classroom behavior; if possible, he wants the parents to endorse his definition and join him in imposing that definition on Davey. Or perhaps he wants to enlist the parents in his battle against Davey. It may be an unjust war, but a surprising number of parents *do* enlist.

Linda Disrupts the Class

"It's hard enough to get a handle on my own child's motivations," one mother told me. "How can I possibly get a handle on the teacher's motivations?" In the pages that follow, you will read about some typical parent-teacher conferences dealing with behavioral problems. These vignettes illustrate how concerned parents can help their children by asking the right questions and learning about the teacher's motivations, attitudes, and defense mechanisms.

Mrs. Bach's classroom walls are plainer than most. She likes the simplicity of bare walls and feels that too much decoration is a distraction to the children. She does not post the children's work on the bulletin boards, because such displays are "too messy." The classroom appears very austere and cold, especially when empty of children.

Mrs. Bach welcomes you and gets straight to the point. Linda, she says, has become a behavior problem. She talks too much and disrupts the class. She lacks self-control and consistently breaks the classroom rules. Mrs. Bach has punished her in various ways—keeping her in from recess, giving her "time out" in the corner, and making her write "I will behave in class" many times. Mrs. Bach has called you in because, despite her efforts at discipline, Linda continues to misbehave.

WHAT'S GOING ON HERE?

If you are like most parents, your first reaction is: "Are we talking about the same kid? That doesn't sound like my child." The child Mrs. Bach is describing is a rotten little kid. If Linda were really a rotten little kid, she'd be rotten all the time—at home and at school. You would have noticed a deep-seated problem in Linda's personality. If she's only rotten some of the time, maybe the fault is in the situation rather than in Linda. In truth, Linda isn't defiant, isn't recalcitrant, and doesn't fit the description that Mrs. Bach paints of her—at least not at home. Of course, you haven't been in the classroom and Mrs.

Bach has; perhaps she is seeing a side of Linda that you haven't ever seen. Or that you have chosen not to see.

WHAT TO ASK THE TEACHER

Mrs. Bach gives the impression that Linda is disruptive all of the time, but that can't be. That is completely inconsistent with the Linda you have seen at home, at Sunday school, in art classes, and at soccer practice. Maybe she is disruptive only during reading time, or when homework is assigned, or when the lesson is boring. You need to ask Mrs. Bach to be specific; when and under what conditions do the disruptions occur? Does the misbehavior involve only Linda, or does it always include other children—perhaps with a particular child? What form does the disruption take? Does Linda display a lack of respect for the teacher or does she consistently violate one of the teacher's rules?

If she is talking, when is she talking? Is she talking to the teacher, to a friend, or to the class? Is she talking about the schoolwork or about unrelated subjects? Is the talking distracting, malicious, disrespectful, or just overly enthusiastic? Ask Mrs. Bach whether the talking is a problem for the class, for Linda's neighbors, for Linda, or just for the teacher.

And be sure to ask Mrs. Bach how much, and under what circumstances, the students are *ever* allowed to speak.

WHAT THE TEACHER IS LIKELY TO SAY . . .
AND WHAT IT MIGHT MEAN

"Normal" behavior and unacceptable behavior are often a matter of personal interpretation. These examples may give you a clearer idea of the teacher's opinions and prejudices.

MRS. BACH: Linda talks too much. If everybody voiced his opinions aloud, the class would be chaotic.

POSSIBLE MEANING: Maintaining order is the top priority for this teacher; everything else, including learning, is secondary. It also means that the teacher thinks that everything from her mouth is more important than anything the students might have to contribute.

The fact is, in the average classroom, 85 percent of the talking is done by the teacher, and only 15 percent is done by all the students together. Clearly, the average teacher doesn't know the difference between teaching and learning. If the teacher would talk less and allow the students to talk more, two things would happen. First, there would be less teaching. Second, there would be more learning. But allowing this kind of creative dialogue would be very hard for teachers like Mrs. Bach, who are afraid of losing control.

MRS. BACH: Linda can't sit still.

POSSIBLE MEANING: You should be very pleased to hear this. It means that she hasn't completely tamed Linda yet, and there is still a lot of spice left in her.

Many teachers confuse action and attention. They think that high activity means low attentiveness, and that inaction is the same as being attentive. These ideas may hold true for adults, but not for children. Clearly, it has been a long time since Mrs. Bach has been a child, or has even understood children.

Often, when a child's interest is attracted to something, her energy level goes up, not down. Engaged in a subject, she may become *more* active rather than less. If the teacher has succeeded in exciting her about a subject, she may not be able to sit still at all. Pensive contemplation is simply not the style of most children.

On the other hand, if the teacher is boring and does nothing to stimulate the child's interest, then the child will find it easier to sit still and vegetate—a condition beloved by teachers who can't tell the difference between rapt and catatonic.

Or the child may become restless. The wise child's mind starts looking for something (anything!) more interesting. When she finds it, she might not sit still. So when Mrs. Bach complains that Linda can't sit still, she is revealing how dull and stultifying her teaching can be.

MRS. BACH: Linda is willfully disruptive.

POSSIBLE MEANING: There are a lot of teachers who don't like children to act like children. They want all their students to act like docile, compliant Little Lord Fauntleroys. If a child shows any signs of life, independent thought, or enthusiasm, the teacher labels it a "behavior problem." Without more in-depth information, you can't just accept a teacher's opinion about the seriousness of the problem. The teacher's specific observations are more valuable to you than her opinions. Ask the teacher: Exactly what is

Linda doing? Why is that a problem? Does Linda tend to misbehave at a specific time of day? During a specific subject? Then ask yourself: Is Linda disruptive at home? When she is in the care of others? When she is engaged in an activity she likes? What rule is she breaking?

ANOTHER POSSIBLE MEANING: Whatever punishment Mrs. Bach has inflicted has not worked. Either she is using ineffective forms of discipline, or she hasn't convinced Linda that her behavior is actually wrong. Ask the teacher: What is Linda's reaction to her punishments? Have you tried other forms of discipline? Does Linda understand this concept: Behavior that is acceptable at home or on the playground may not be acceptable in your classroom?

MRS. BACH: Linda may have an emotional problem.

POSSIBLE MEANING: Teachers are quick to jump to the conclusion that bad behavior is a symptom of emotional or psychological problems. Teachers are not trained psychologists; nor should they play at being headshrinkers. At most schools, the teachers are categorically prohibited from citing emotional problems or recommending psychological testing or counseling. Only the school administration is allowed to do so, and then only when following specific guidelines.

So how do you respond to Mrs. Bach's comments about Linda? First, get the facts. Ignore her generalized comments about Linda's demeanor and attitude and find out exactly what she has done and under exactly what conditions. Then judge for yourself whether Linda's behavior is abnormal, normal but inappropriate for the classroom, or normal but not acceptable to this teacher.

If her behavior has been abnormal, get help; Mrs. Bach is not allowed to jump to psychological conclusions, but you are.

If Linda's behavior is normal but inappropriate for the classroom, cooperate with Mrs. Bach in changing Linda's behavior.

But if the problem lies with Mrs. Bach, if you feel that her classroom is too repressive for normal children like Linda, then you do not want to cooperate in the subjugation of your child. Question the rigidity of her rules; question the way they are imposed on the children; question the appropriateness of the rules for various situations; question the effect that her discipline has on the children; and question the effectiveness of her punishments on Linda and on others. Put her on the defensive, because that is where she should be.

Teachers like Mrs. Bach want you to join her in her battle against your own child; you can't do that. On the other hand, you can't join Linda in the battle against Mrs. Bach either. What you need to do is to keep asking both sides, "Why are you fighting? Can't you find a way to get along?" Encourage Linda to avoid irritating Mrs. Bach (even when Mrs. Bach is wrong); and discourage Mrs. Bach from being so repressive (by making her justify each level of repression).

HOW LONG BEFORE YOU CAN EXPECT RESULTS

With some problems, the results can be immediate. If Linda is a good girl without any underlying problems, occasional naughtiness can be dealt with quickly. Chances are, she was just rattling her cage. A firm response from a united front of parents and teachers should be enough to convince her to reform.

Most children want to behave, and they will behave if the whole classroom understands the need for rules and accepts those rules. Sometimes a refresher course on "living within a society's rules" is helpful for the whole class, and may resolve Linda's problem . . . for a while.

But if Linda has a serious behavior problem that will require psychological counseling, it won't be solved quickly. It's important to note that the problem won't solve itself, and that the solution won't come until you start actively looking for it. Since Linda is relying on you to help her put an end to her school conflicts, you need to work with the teacher to define the problem and decide how to help.

If, on the other hand, you feel that the *teacher* has a serious problem that has an emotional impact on Linda, the solution does not lie with you. Nothing you do will solve the problem. So you will have to make a choice— either help Linda get through the year with this teacher, or get Linda out of that classroom. Later chapters of the book will help you with this dilemma.

Randy Fights with Other Kids

You have come for your first conference with Randy's teacher, Mr. Garrett. Mr. Garrett explains that he has asked for this conference because Randy was in a fight, and the other boy went home with a bloody lip. The other parents were very upset, especially after they found out that this was not the first time Randy had been in a fight.

WHAT'S GOING ON HERE?

You aren't surprised to hear about the fight; Randy had already told you about it, and showed you the tear in the knee of his jeans. He had fought with a boy who had been alternately a friend and an enemy for months, and was now a friend again.

You were not aware of a whole series of fights, and you never thought of Randy as an angry or aggressive child. He never fought with other children, either at your home or other homes; and he never fought at the parks and playgrounds. It is surprising to find that he is fighting at school, and you wonder why his behavior is different there. You are glad of the opportunity to meet with the teacher and find out more about this situation, and about the teacher.

You wonder whether Randy is learning from Mr. Garrett to be combative and confrontational. Randy has come home with several conflicting descriptions of him. Some days he is cheerful and enthusiastic, and some days he is irritable and depressed. And some days he swings from one mood to another without warning. You think he may be manic-depressive, but then everybody has different moods, and his mood swings may only be a slight exaggeration of your own, so how can you cast the first stone?

You have seen the reflection of Mr. Garrett's moods in your own child, and there have been mornings when you wondered what mood he would bring home with him that day. Since Randy, like most kids, is such a good conductor of his teacher's temperamental swings, it isn't impossible that something in Mr. Garrett's room, or even Mr. Garrett himself, may be causing Randy's aggression.

WHAT TO ASK THE TEACHER

You know your own child, and you haven't seen anything inherently aggressive about him. You need to find out more about the classroom climate: Is there anything in that situation that brings out the fighter in Randy?

Ask the teacher whether Randy is involved in all of the fights, or if other children fight with each other. Maybe the whole atmosphere is malignant, or maybe Randy is more noticeable only because he *wins* his fights.

Ask the teacher whether there is a general problem with teasing and taunting. Among the girls, is there a pattern of forming groups for the purpose of excluding one girl?

Ask the teacher about the classroom—is the work there competitive or cooperative? Healthy in-class competition can manifest itself in less healthy ways in the school yard. Are there opportunities for assigned group work, and how well does that go? Ask the teacher about the playground—does he supervise? Does he see the same interactions there as in the classroom?

WHAT THE TEACHER IS LIKELY TO SAY . . .
AND WHAT IT MIGHT MEAN

Fighting is a serious problem, and uncovering the reason for aggressive behavior in children requires serious consideration. These hints can help.

MR. GARRETT: Randy fights with the other kids.
POSSIBLE MEANING: The other kids also fight with Randy, since it takes two to make a fight. Even if Randy is involved in

all the fights, it doesn't mean that Randy started the fights. Maybe there is a group that doesn't like Randy. Maybe there is a game to see how far Randy can be pushed before he fights back. Maybe there is a game to get Randy in trouble with the teacher. Maybe Randy is so oppressed by some adult at school, that he has to lash out at something.

MR. GARRETT: Randy is a troublemaker.

POSSIBLE MEANING: Every year in Mr. Garrett's class, there is always one boy who is tagged "the bad boy." Because that child—at least in Mr. Garrett's mind—is thoroughly exasperating and badly behaved, Mr. Garrett is able to justify his tendency to focus his anger on that one child. Randy may have been selected "troublemaker of the year."

But even if Randy escapes being this year's target, he's not completely safe. If he comes home from school day after day and reports, "Mr. Garrett got mad at Tommy again," then Tommy has a problem. And Mr. Garrett has a problem. And although Tommy is not your child, you have a problem, too. Tommy could be looking to make Randy the new scapegoat and actively trying to get him in trouble. Your child may be living in fear that he may become Mr. Garrett's next target. He is also learning wrong ideas about personal relationships and about problem-solving techniques.

WHAT TO DO

Make it clear to the teacher that you value his observations, so you can get at the facts, but make it equally clear that, in the absence of facts, you are not ready to accept his conclusions about Randy. His opinion that Randy is a troublemaker is just that, an opinion. It is not an established fact, it does not define the problem, and it does not suggest a solution. It may be established that Randy fought, but you don't even know whether he was attacking others or defending himself. Or he may have been standing up for some principle we all believe in. And until you know why he fought, you cannot form a course of action; nor can you punish Randy.

You and Mr. Garrett could teach Randy how to resolve disputes without resorting to fighting, but that won't solve the problem if Randy is so busy defending himself that he can't conciliate his attackers.

If you suspect that Randy has been selected by Mr. Garrett as troublemaker of the year, you must proceed very delicately. Without being confrontational, you must give Mr. Garrett the impression that you are very sympathetic to his problems, and that you want *all* the details so you can deal with Randy properly. For any problem that involves Randy, you want details on the people, circumstances, and causes of the conflict. It is often very productive to have discussions with parents of the other children involved.

HOW LONG BEFORE YOU CAN EXPECT RESULTS

Children don't like to fight, so most of these problems are resolved quickly. As soon as Randy discovers that fighting has consequences that involve the teacher, his parents, and possibly the principal and other parents, he generally loses interest in fighting.

However, if the core of the problem is a serious emotional dysfunction in either Randy or the teacher, it will not be resolved quickly. Some children find that conflict is their most satisfying form of personal interaction, so they invite or provoke confrontation. It may require a long process, probably involving a psychiatrist, to retrain these children in better ways of relating to others.

Recently, school districts have begun to "mainstream" emotionally handicapped children by placing them in regular classrooms like Randy's. If the core of the problem is a dysfunctional classmate, there are immediate ways to lessen that child's impact on Randy and the other children. But the threat will continue as long as the dysfunctional child remains in that classroom.

Maintaining Your Composure in the Conference

When there is a classroom behavioral problem, a good teacher wants to fix the problem; a bad teacher wants to affix blame. The good teacher will ask for a conference and will give the parents all the facts beforehand, so the parents can come to the conference well prepared. The bad teacher will delay or avoid the parent conference. When pressed, the bad teacher will schedule the conference but not give the parents enough information to prepare for it. This is an "ambush" conference, one in which the teacher has already decided to affix blame on your child, and wants you unprepared to defend him. The ambush conference is more likely when the teacher has been at fault or in some way inadequate, and is trying to shift blame away from himself.

The intent of the ambush conference is to put you on the defensive, but the result may be to leave you in tears or to incite you to anger. Although your anger and frustration would be entirely justified, either reaction is a victory for the teacher and a loss for your child.

I suggest that you take a deep breath, perhaps adjourn to the hallway for a drink of water, and resolve to stay calm. The conference has already given you a firsthand look at what your child may be experiencing every day. Nevertheless, it would be a mistake to counterattack at this point. You have no ammunition. You have no information about what your son or daughter did or didn't do, or why. And even if you did, arguing with the teacher would not help. Counterattacking at this point would only raise the teacher's defenses, and close off your avenues of information gathering. If the teacher is a very bad one, she might react to your anger by taking out her own frustrations on your child, in subtle or overt ways.

Rather than bursting into tears or lashing out in anger, your response to the teacher should be, "Let's accept, for the purposes of discussion, that what you say about my daughter is true. Now what can we do to improve the situation?" That cuts to the heart of the matter. It also requires the teacher to stop blaming and start thinking constructively.

Finally, don't agree to any suggestions from the teacher about punishing your child. Punishment is rarely constructive; other forms of discipline have proven more effective than punishment. Besides, your child's "guilt" has not been established yet except for "purposes of discussion." Give your child the benefit of the doubt.

A Final Checklist

This chapter has suggested numerous questions that parents might ask in order to gather more information about their child and their child's classroom. None of the questions is designed to put a teacher on the defensive, and good teachers will not feel threatened by these questions. Good teachers recognize that parents are concerned and want to be involved in their children's education. When they hear such questions, good teachers will make a mental note that "Here is a concerned parent. I had better keep an eye out for this child, so I will be prepared to answer their detailed questions next time."

On the other hand, when you ask detailed questions of a bad teacher, the response will be different. She may behave as though she has something to hide, or resort to the grade book for her answers. She may sigh loudly, as though she resents having to think about your child more than superficially. She may look at her watch, indicate irritation, check the door to see whether her next appointment is waiting, and otherwise try to make the parents uncomfortable so they will stop asking questions and go away. Don't go away!

The person who requested the conference usually sets the agenda for the conference. If the teacher called for the conference, she may expect to make her points and then adjourn the meeting. But you have an agenda, too, regardless of who called the conference. Don't be shoved out the door until all five of these criteria have been met:

1. You and the teacher agree on the definition of the problem—at least, until you have exchanged opinions on the possible definition of the problem.
2. You have acquired a sense of the classroom atmosphere and the student-teacher interactions that occur there.
3. You and the teacher have agreed on a plan of action. You are clear about what you must do, the

teacher is clear about what she must do, and you both are clear about what you expect the child to do.

4. You have brought the child into the conference and into the plan. *He* is clear about what he must do.
5. You have set a reasonable and realistic date for a follow-up meeting to review the child's progress.

A cordial but confident demeanor, an unwavering refusal to blame the child, and an arsenal of challenging questions send a powerful message to the teacher. They let the teacher know that you care about your child, that you will defend your child, and that her opinions need to be backed up by facts. A good teacher, or one who needs to be reminded to be good, will change her attitude toward your child in the face of such parental strength. But a bad teacher either will not or cannot change.

If the process of ferreting out the bad teacher begins at the conference, it begins to develop depth after the conference—particularly if the conference has made no difference in the relationship between the teacher and child, and has made no difference in the child's progress.

Remember those articles you have read about the "ideal parent-teacher conference"? Did you notice that they never suggest what to do when the conference goals are not met? They never even recognize that such an outcome is possible!

But it is possible. You may not be dealing with the superteacher who wrote the articles. You may be dealing with an inferior teacher, one who can't even recognize your child's problem, much less solve it. What does happen, in real life, when the conference goals are not met? The next chapter will tell you what such a failure says about the child's problem—and about the child's teacher.

4

When the Conference Is Over but the Misery Lingers On

Several weeks have passed since your conference with your daughter Miranda's teacher. At that time, you and the teacher had carefully drafted a plan that, the teacher assured you, would solve Miranda's problems. Since then, you have done everything the plan required of you, and you made sure that Miranda has done her part, too.

Naturally, you have been expecting Miranda's behavior and achievement to improve, but so far that hasn't happened. In fact, some things have gotten worse. Her homework grades have been better, and as far as you can tell, overall comprehension of the material has improved; but at the end of the marking period, Miranda's test results are just as dismal as ever. As for Miranda's behavior, it improved for about three days. She has since regressed to the same old stuff—she is apathetic and sullen. Even though she seems to sleep more than before, it's harder to get her up in the morning.

At three o'clock, the school bell is like a whistling teakettle, signifying pent-up pressure that needs to be released now. Miranda explodes out of the schoolhouse, rips through her toys, and provokes arguments with her siblings and friends. She is resistant to your helpful suggestions and she doesn't respond to your attempts at positive reinforcement. She is calling for help and resisting it at the same time.

Miranda is frustrated. At the conference, you and the teacher emphasized to Miranda how the plan was going to help her. She seemed to accept the plan, and did her best to adhere to it, albeit without much visible excitement. After a very few days, Miranda didn't see any improvement; all she saw was parents and teacher ganging up on her. Miranda doesn't look at the plan as a way of making her better; she sees it as the official recognition that parents and teacher think she's stupid. She also views the plan more as punishment than healing prescription. She figures that if she's going to do the time, she might as well do the crime, and her attitude and behavior are worse than ever.

Miranda doesn't want to tell you about her day in school, because the more you know, the more she will get "planned" and programmed out of her free time. She doesn't even want to tell you about field trips and recess. Her revelations will only cement the link between you and the teacher. With the two of you happily "in cahoots" with each other, Miranda feels alone and isolated. Who is on her side?

Of course, you are frustrated, too. The plan seemed logical when the teacher outlined it, and you are holding up your end. Assuming that you diagnosed the problem correctly and devised a good plan, why isn't the plan working? The weak link in the chain has to be in the classroom. Something is happening, or not happening, there that is bad for Miranda. You need to know more about the atmosphere in the classroom, the way the students interact with the teacher and with each other. Most of all, you need to know who isn't making the grade—Miranda or her teacher.

Your Eyes and Ears in the Classroom

"What I wouldn't give to be a fly on the wall, so I could see what really goes on in Miss Smith's classroom." Every parent has said this at some time in a child's education. It's so natural to wonder if your child behaves the same when you are not around to watch her. Does she interact with other children differently if she thinks that you aren't there? Wouldn't it be fun to observe? And if Miranda is struggling in school, it becomes more than just fun; it becomes critical. You need to know what is happening in the classroom.

If you are like most people, you can identify one special teacher who influenced your life in a positive way. And if you are like most people, you can point to another teacher who made you feel stupid, insecure, or insignificant. If you crossed paths with that teacher in high school, you might have been angry with her for making you feel bad. But if you were exposed to that belittling, insensitive teacher in elementary school, you probably accepted her opinion and thought of yourself as stupid, insecure, or insignificant. Little children tend to live up to the expectations of the adults who are significant to them. It never occurs to them to question whether the teacher might be wrong.

Nor does it occur to them to question the teacher's

ability. Elementary school children don't know a good teacher from a bad one. Their memory doesn't carry well from one year to the next, and even if it did, they wouldn't have enough experience to compare teachers. They know whether they liked a teacher, but they don't know whether she was skilled—or even interested. If they have a teacher who demeans them, they simply assume that that is normal for that grade in school. If they are struggling, they assume they aren't smart enough to "get" the lesson.

They aren't likely to blame the teacher and, because they are feeling guilty, they don't want to tell their parents about what happened at school. What is worse, if the teacher is treating them badly, they assume it is because they have inadvertently done something to deserve mistreatment.

The child's tendency is to keep the various parts of her life separate (children are dumbfounded when they happen upon their teacher in the grocery store, or anywhere away from the school), and some try hard to maintain walls between the separate parts. Nevertheless, with effort, you can get beyond the blockade, extract the information you need about classroom climate, and discover whether the *teacher* is following the agreed-upon plan, or whether she is just biding time until she can pass Miranda on to the next teacher. All you need to do is get into the classroom, get into the flow of parent-to-parent information, or get into Miranda's mode of communication.

MAKE YOURSELF A PART OF THE CLASSROOM

The most direct way to find out what's happening in the classroom is to go to the school and see the interaction for yourself.

Permission to visit classrooms may vary from state to state, district to district, school to school. Visits may be limited by bureaucratic regulations in the state educational code, school district policies, or individual school policies. If you ask the teacher in advance (tell her you intend to observe Miranda, not her!), and if she is amenable to your visit, you might be able to ignore silly rules. If the teacher seems agreeable but cites a school rule against classroom visitors, tell the teacher that you will ask the principal to waive the rule and allow you a (short) visit. Sometimes a note on a letterhead from a child psychologist is helpful in getting a waiver.

If the teacher is opposed to having visitors, then you need to wonder why. The best teachers welcome parental involvement, so it is entirely possible that the teacher has something to hide. If school policy prohibits visits, then you must question the administrator's motives for keeping you out. Maybe the school has something to hide. On the other hand, some schools are so exemplary that they are besieged with constant requests from prospective parents and educators who want to observe their stellar program. In this case, excessive visits from outsiders could interfere with the educational program, so they make rules restricting classroom observation. Those rules, however, should not limit observation by parents of *currently enrolled* children.

Another way of getting into the classroom is to volunteer your services. Offer to lend a hand with slow readers, the library, grading papers, taking attendance, collecting money for class trips, or whatever opportunity is offered to you. Bear in mind, however, that recurring volunteer service will serve your purpose better than a single classroom visit. A single scheduled visit allows a teacher to create an artificial scene in which she and the students display their best behavior. By visiting repeatedly and without calling attention to yourself, you gradually become a part of the furniture. When Miranda, her classmates, and the teacher no longer notice that you are there, then you can observe the classroom as it really is.

Observe the way the teacher interacts with the students. Does he call on some students more than others—for example, on boys more than girls? Does he call on the noisy ones or the quiet ones? Does he encourage participation from the reticent? How does he respond to the children's wrong answers? Does he reassure some, chastise some, and ignore others? Does he encourage civility in the way children treat each other?

Most of all, how does he treat Miranda? Does he seem sympathetic to Miranda's needs, or just irritated by her problems? In your parent-teacher conference, you had created a plan to help Miranda improve, and that plan called for certain things to occur in the classroom. Are those things happening? Is Miranda getting individual attention? Is there a record of her daily progress and behavior? Has her seating or grouping been changed? Is she getting positive reinforcement from the teacher?

SPEAK TO OTHER PARENTS

Word of mouth is the best advertisement. You get your information from someone you know and trust, someone who has already tried the product, someone who has no reason to gloss over its flaws.

Similarly, if you want to know the real scoop about Miranda's teacher, ask other parents. Any parent whose child was recently in Mr. Duplin's class—whether that child's experience was positive or negative—will have some information that is useful to you. Those parents have had the opportunity you have not had: a full year to make observations about how Mr. Duplin treats his students. They will know how he deals with children just like Miranda. They will be more aware of Mr. Duplin's quirks and idiosyncrasies. They will know how Miranda can avoid lighting the teacher's short fuse, and when she should run for cover.

Other parents can also be sources of good advice that may illuminate *your* dealings with the teacher. How does she respond to parent's comments and suggestions? Is the teacher likely to follow through on plans? Does she have a history of providing individual attention when needed? What has happened to children whose parents found it necessary to appeal to the principal? How has she treated students whose parents have requested a transfer to another class? These are questions that are rarely answered honestly by administrators and other teachers—only other parents will give you a straight answer.

It is important, however, that you get your information from more than one parent. It is always possible that one parent has an unfounded prejudice against a teacher, so it is best to form a consensus. And in talking to various parents, make it clear that you are just gathering information. Don't act the part of the disgruntled parent— even if you are one. Word may get back to the school administrators, and you may get a reputation as a troublemaker. Once you have been so labeled, you aren't apt to get any more information. And you are less likely to succeed in getting Miranda the help she needs.

LISTEN TO WHAT YOUR CHILD MAY BE
TRYING TO TELL YOU

Children can be creatures of deep feelings and few words. I remember seeing on the television news a story about a child snatched from the jaws of death by a gallant passerby. Asked what he thought of the brave hero who risked life and limb to come to his aid, the child shrugged his shoulders and said, "He's nice." If your child is less than ten years old, that's the same response you get when you ask him about his teacher: "She's nice." *Nice* is a mild positive that communicates absolutely nothing. If there were a response that communicated even less information, the child would probably use that instead. Children will tell you what you want to hear; and if they aren't sure what you want, they will temporize with a meaningless response like *nice* until you give them more definite signals.

Every parent of a struggling child wants to know what's going on in the classroom. And every parent has been frustrated in attempts to extract meaningful information from the child about that classroom. The struggling child associates guilt and embarrassment with school; he wants to leave the pain in the classroom, and not be forced to think about it elsewhere. Even if he were willing to talk about it, the primary school–aged child doesn't have the vocabulary to do so. Indeed, it is a rare second-grader who is able to provide his parent with a detailed personality profile of the teacher, or to give an in-depth appraisal of his daily interactions with her.

As a parent, you have to maximize whatever scraps of information your child offers about classroom life. The problem is in getting your son or daughter to provide you with those scraps. In my work, I have used the technique of "reflection"; it has been widely parodied in the media, but it still works on children. A conversation using the reflection technique might go something like this:

Ralph: "Tommy got in trouble again."

Mom: "You say Tommy got in trouble again."

Note that all you've done is repeat Ralph's statement back to him, without adding any judgments or comments of your own. By inflecting your voice slightly upward on the last syllable, you offer Ralph the opportunity to say more about the incident. Because you haven't made a judgment about Tommy, or the teacher, or jumped to any conclusions about your own child's possible involvement, Ralph feels free to say more about it.

Ralph: "Yeah, Tommy and Joey were talking and the teacher yelled at Tommy."

Mom: "The teacher yelled at Tommy."

If Ralph never volunteers information about the class, you need to ask questions as unobtrusively as possible. Probe for details rather than opinions, and start with questions that don't directly involve Ralph. For example, don't ask, "How was reading class today?" Instead, ask "What does the teacher do with the other reading group? What does she do with your group?" Don't ask, "Did your teacher tell you how to subtract with borrowing?" It would be more effective to ask, "How did she tell you . . ." You will be able to draw more conclusions from details than from adjectives and one-word answers.

PICKING UP ON YOUR CHILD'S MESSAGES

Picture a child, perhaps your child, up to his neck and struggling to stay afloat in a bad classroom situation with a bad teacher. The child is drowning and has no idea that it isn't his fault. He is small and inarticulate and he feels inadequate. He is afraid that his parents will be angry with him for his imagined flaws, so he doesn't want to tell them. Still, he has to do something, so he throws out a note in a bottle, hoping that someone somewhere will find the note and rescue him. The longer the problem continues, the more bottles are thrown out.

Look for the bottles. They are the chance comments, tossed off the cuff, that tell you what is on Ralph's mind and what he really thinks about school. They can speak volumes about his teachers. The following sketches illustrate some common teacher types that you may recognize, along with the comments that your child might make as he tries to cope with those teachers.

Mrs. Gray has been at Water Street School for so long, she has her own parking place. It doesn't really have her name on it, but it's just sort of accepted that her full-sized gray Buick cruises past all the Toyotas and Escorts and settles majestically into the place next to the principal's space. Another perk of seniority is her full-time teacher's aide, who actually does most of the work. Mrs. Gray is so near retirement, she is using her accumulated sick days and vacation days; she is rarely there on Mondays, and often skips Friday, too.

YOUR CHILD SAYS: "Mrs. Gray didn't check last night's math homework. Mrs. Gray wasn't there again today."

WHAT IT MEANS: Your child is at the mercy of an absentee teacher. Although you may have worked out an agreeable plan with the teacher, the teacher is not there to implement it. Your child gets no feedback on his daily work and therefore has no idea what he is doing wrong or how to do it right.

Olivia Blevins is a dedicated teacher. She has a genuine affection for and rapport with the children, and she wants to do the very best she can. But some of the children are struggling, and Miss Blevins hasn't a clue why, because she has never learned anything about detecting learning differences among students. Miss Blevins is an experienced teacher. She should realize that if a child is doing badly in school, there is always a reason, and the reason is rarely laziness or willfulness. She should recognize that some children learn by listening, some by seeing, and some by feeling; and her classroom surely contains children of each learning style. She should understand that some children are facile with words, some with numbers, and some with neither; and that children vary widely in the amount of time needed to absorb knowledge.

Most of all, she should know enough about specific learning disorders to detect the symptoms of visual problems, hearing problems, perceptual problems, motor problems, and the various other problems that keep children from success.

YOUR CHILD SAYS: "She went over it with me a hundred times, but I still don't get it."

WHAT IT MEANS: Your child is doing the best she can, but the plan you and the teacher agreed on is not working. There is something keeping your child from learning, and it is something beyond her control and beyond her understanding. She needs someone's sympathetic ear and analytical mind.

Mr. Griffin believes that clear, orderly handwriting is the sign of a clear, orderly mind. Consequently, he gives lower grades to children who have poor handwriting, because he associates it with poor organization and poor effort.

A child may be plagued by handwriting that is too clumsy to keep pace with his fine, quick brain. In writing, the child may leave out words, sentences, and entire ideas because his hand hasn't developed the fine motor skills to keep up with his thoughts. The child begins to substitute short, easy words for the more complex, precise words because they are easier to write. The student's fluency and creativity are stifled by the need to get something legible onto paper; and then Mr. Griffin's assumption—that poor handwriting is a symptom of overall poor effort—becomes a self-fulfilling prophecy.

YOUR CHILD SAYS: "He wouldn't grade my paper. He wants me to do it over . . . again."

WHAT IT MEANS: Your child is frustrated by a teacher who won't recognize his strengths, who only focuses on his weaknesses. His teacher's priorities are out of order, but your child can't tell him that. There needs to be some change in the teacher's remediation plan, or the teacher's attitude, before your child gives up altogether on trying to please him.

Mrs. Stein starts each school year by reading the "permanent record" folders for each of her new students. This allows her to pick up "right where the class left off in June." It also allows her to pick up on her predecessor's prejudices against those students she has identified as the lazy ones and the troublemakers (you know, the ones you have to watch like a hawk before they try anything) and focus on the smart ones (the ones you must cultivate carefully to help them blossom).

YOUR CHILD SAYS: "She never calls on me. She treats me just like my teacher last year. Why should I even try?"

WHAT IT MEANS: You can disregard anything the teacher told you at the conference about giving your child a fresh start. Your child has been typecast, based on the way she was a year ago. She never got the chance to start the year with a clean slate.

Mr. Lawrence is a teacher with a mission. He wants to teach his students the right way to live, whether they like it or not. Mr. Lawrence loves all of his students . . . no, he loves most of his students, but he feels enormous guilt about not loving the others.

Mr. Lawrence has a heightened sense of "the way things are supposed to be." There is little doubt in his mind about what is right and what is wrong. He is judgmental and disapproving about other teachers' habits and lifestyles. While this characteristic may not add to Mr. Lawrence's popularity in the teacher's lounge, he is quite compatible with his fourth- and fifth-graders, who

also ignore shades of gray and tend to prefer moral abso-
lutes.

Mr. Lawrence's classes are some of the school's best
. . . at least when it comes to sitting up straight, marching
in straight lines, and behaving at lunchtime. The chil-
dren have also become adept at figuring out what answer
Mr. Lawrence wants and feeding it back to him. They do
well on true-false tests and multiple-choice tests, but they
can't write essays. They can tell you what and when, but
they can't tell you why. They can't answer open-ended
questions, and they panic at rhetorical questions.

Mr. Lawrence is highly regarded at Water Street
School. The principal sees a line of well-behaved children
and assumes that Mr. Lawrence is one of her best teach-
ers. The parents who visit the classroom are always im-
pressed at how orderly the class seems. But they wonder
why their children, who are so well behaved at school,
need to blow off steam when they get home.

YOUR CHILD SAYS: "The classes are so long, and he won't let us
talk. If I make one mistake, he makes me do it over. And
he favors the girls."

WHAT IT MEANS: Despite any promises from Mr. Lawrence that
he would do all he could to engage your child, his classes
seem long because they are so boring, and the assigned
work is repetitive and uninteresting. It may be that your
child is trying to cope with a control freak. Mr. Lawrence
will make him feel guilty about any action that doesn't
match his preconceived expectations. He expects all the
children, even the normally active small boys, to act like
docile little robots.

Mrs. Clark is using the district's new "diagnostic-prescriptive" reading program for the primary grades. In order to comply with the program, Mrs. Clark must constantly test the children to measure their mastery of the hundreds of little steps that make up the reading process. Since most of Mrs. Clark's time is taken up with testing and record keeping, very little time is left for actual teaching. Still, Mrs. Clark feels very professional, the kids are always busy, the parents are getting detailed information about each child's reading level, and everyone feels that the program is a big success, except for one thing: The students aren't learning.

YOUR CHILD SAYS: "I hate reading! It's so boring."

WHAT IT MEANS: Your child is getting "programmed" out of his natural love of reading. The school has succeeded in taking something that was *fun,* and making it into something that is *work.*

Mr. Welton is teaching math and the children are learning—but they are not learning math. They are learning to hate school, to hate math, and to hate Mr. Welton. While Mr. Welton is busy teaching math, the children are absorbing the message that being a learner means being a bored, silent, repressed drone. It is no wonder so many of Mr. Welton's students hate school.

Mr. Welton can't help it. He is only doing what he was trained to do. Mr. Welton's teacher training classes focused on methodology—the "How to Teach Arithmetic" course, the "How to Teach Reading" course, and so on. He was taught that if he follows the approved method, he will be an approved teacher. The assumption is that children can learn only if the approved teaching method is used.

YOUR CHILD SAYS (in a torrent of tears): "No! Mr. Welton says you aren't supposed to help us! We have to do it his way!"

WHAT IT MEANS: Mr. Welton is probably a young teacher, one not bright enough to question what he was taught in teacher's college. He may have an exaggerated opinion of his own role in the learning process, and too low an opinion of the role of parents. The remedial plan he is enacting is not helping your child, and he is preventing you from helping—if you follow his rules.

Your child's comments are telling you that his needs are still not being met in the classroom. He is also letting you know that you need to go out and look for the root of the problem. It would not be unreasonable to look more closely at your child's teacher. After all, a million elementary school children have to deal with incompetent teachers every year. Still, there are other factors that might be at work in your child's situation. And although in the meantime you must offer your child unconditional support and help—as if the teacher *were* to blame for his difficulties—you shouldn't jump hastily to the conclusion that the teacher is at fault until all the factors have been explored.

5

Learning Difficulties

Covering All the Bases

Here is a nightmare for you. Imagine yourself in a heated conference with the school principal. You have fire in your eyes and steam coming out of your ears. You are citing chapter and verse of the teacher's misdeeds, and raking the teacher over the coals for his insensitivity and intolerance. After you play your role as your child's defender, you sit back in your seat, waiting to pounce on whatever poor excuse the principal chooses to offer for the teacher's poor performance. Instead, he calmly puts out your fire. The teacher has discovered that Jenny's problems may be due to a hearing deficiency (or visual or some other specific problem). You feel very foolish.

Before you storm in to the principal's office, you must be very, very sure that the problem lies with the teacher, and not with your own child. Granted, the teacher should be skilled enough to recognize specific learning difficulties, but you can't rely upon that. Many teachers don't know what to look for. Others don't look at all.

The truth is, if Jenny has a specific learning difficulty,

it may be up to you to find it. And that isn't easy. Learning difficulty is a huge topic, and many excellent books have been written about it. Learning difficulties are also quite complex and therefore hard to pinpoint or diagnose— even for professionals. Consequently, this book does not intend to cover the subject in detail. Instead, we will describe typical symptoms of the most common learning difficulties and explain how these difficulties can masquerade as academic or behavioral problems, so that you can make an informed decision about whether your child needs to be evaluated professionally, in order to get him the help he needs.

Learning difficulties are categorized as input, processing, or output problems. *Input problems* interfere with getting information into the child's brain—that is, problems with his vision or hearing. *Processing problems* are flaws in the way he perceives, organizes, and stores information *after* it has entered his brain. *Output problems* show up in the way he expresses information—that is, problems with his speaking and writing. It should be noted that, in a real child, the problems rarely fit into a single one of these three categories.

Input Problems

VISUAL

Acuity: The most common eye difficulty is a problem with acuity, an inability to focus clearly. Objects that are well defined to the normal eye appear fuzzy to a child with poor acuity. A child who is nearsighted has perfect vision of things near her face, but objects in the distance are blurry. This problem is easy to detect *if you are look-ing for it* but may go undetected for years if you don't inquire. After all, the child has no idea that her images are fuzzy.

Symptoms: Say to Jenny, "Look at those stars!" If she can't see as many stars as you see, then she may have a problem. Or say, "Read that billboard over there." If she can't see the words you see, then there's a problem. If she asks, "What billboard?" then you have a big problem. If Jenny, while reading a book, holds it very close to her face, you should have her checked for nearsightedness.

In the classroom: A nearsighted child may have trouble seeing details on the blackboard. If the teacher's usual method is to explain the lessons at the blackboard, he may have trouble understanding the lesson, and may be perceived as inattentive or stupid. He may compensate by asking the teacher for a one-to-one repetition of the lesson; teachers lose patience with this very quickly, saying, "Why didn't you pay attention the first time?" Homework assignments pose another problem for the nearsighted child, because many teachers write the as-signments on the board. The child may not notice the as-signment, or may miss page numbers or other details of the assignment.

What the good teacher will do to help: A sensitive teacher should recognize that the child has a problem with nearsightedness. Some children may give a clue of the problem by squinting, but teachers should not wait for such obvious symptoms. It is not difficult or time con-suming for the teacher to give all her students a simple screening by having them read from the blackboard early in the school year. Children with vision problems should be seated near the blackboard and near the teacher.

Farsightedness: Another type of acuity problem is farsightedness. A child may be able to read billboards very well, but things near him (such as books) appear fuzzy. This is a problem that is much more common among adults of middle age, but it is not unknown among children.

Symptoms: If Jenny holds her book far away when she reads, farsightedness is a possibility. If she can make out details far away but has trouble reading from a book, have her vision checked.

Astigmatism: Another type of acuity problem is astigmatism. It may exist by itself or in combination with other acuity problems. Astigmatism is caused by a flaw in the lens of the eye, and the result is also a fuzzy image. But in this case the fuzziness is in only a part of the vision, or only in lines running in one direction but not another.

Symptoms: The child may be able to see most letters very clearly, but letters with certain diagonal elements might appear fuzzy, or the diagonal elements might just disappear. An R might look like a P, for example.

In the classroom: The child can't learn certain letters, no matter how hard he tries. He can't seem to apply the phonics he has learned. Of course, the child doesn't know that his vision is any different from the next child's; he doesn't know why everyone else can distinguish the letters and he can't. The child assumes he is stupid, and the teacher assumes the same.

What the good teacher will do to help: The sensitive teacher should look for vision problems. If a child is confusing certain letters, the teacher might try the same letters in a different typeface, or have the child read the letters while holding the material at different angles. If problems are noted, the teacher should recommend that parents get further testing for their child.

Here are some other visual input problems to look out for:

Accommodation: The eye has to adjust its focus when it turns its gaze from a near object to a far object. This is called the accommodation reflex, and we do it without thinking about it. Sometimes, deep in thought, we turn our heads without changing our eye focus. Gazing into the middle distance, we might not see things that are right before our eyes.

Symptoms: Daydreamers and children often spend a lot of time gazing into the middle distance. It probably doesn't indicate a weakness in the accommodation reflex, but it doesn't hurt to check. If your child seems slow in focusing his eyes when he turns his head, have a specialist evaluate his accommodation reflex. If the child has trouble catching a ball, it could be a motor problem, but it could be a weakness in the visual accommodation reflex.

In the classroom: A child with poor accommodation may have trouble in copying things off the board or writing answers to questions on the board. Any activity that involves repetitive shifting of vision from the paper to the teacher and back again might be difficult for this child.

Illumination: Another automatic reflex is the way the eye adjusts to different light conditions. When you move from bright sunlight into a darkened room, your eye's illumination reflex widens the pupils so you can see.

This is another ability that tends to decline with age. Older people may have difficulty driving at night, because their eyes adjust too slowly to oncoming headlights. But most children have an excellent illumination reflex.

Binocular Fusion: The eyes usually work in pairs. This has the benefit of an effective fail-safe system, in case one of the eyes develops a problem, either temporary or permanent. Also, the two-eye system gives us our depth perception. But there are also potential problems in the two-eye system.

A child with binocular fusion problems may have 20/20 vision in each eye, but he can't get both eyes to focus and get the same image from each.

Symptoms: A child with this problem has trouble keeping both eyes focused on a moving object. It may appear, at times, that his two eyes are not looking at the same object. Sometimes a child has a "wandering eye" (quite a different problem from a man's wandering eye). The child may have one eye in which the muscles are not as well developed as in the other eye. The weaker eye has trouble keeping focus on a moving object. The child gets in the habit of using the good eye exclusively, and the weaker eye never does develop properly. When you see a young child with a single eye patch, it is often a treatment for this problem. The "good" eye is covered, forcing the weaker eye to do all the work and thereby develop itself.

In the classroom: Less obvious problems of binocular fusion may not be detected in the preschool years, and may only surface as the child is learning to read. At this point, binocular fusion problems may have a major impact on the child's schoolwork, and are certain to harm the child's attitude toward reading.

When we read, our eyes travel across a line of type; then they shift down one line and to the left for another line of type. While we read, we normally read with one eye or the other. We unconsciously shift back and forth between right eye and left eye as we read. For children with good binocular fusion, this is an easy, automatic process.

For a child with poor binocular fusion, reading is a struggle. Every time she makes an automatic shift from one eye to the other, something bad happens. Either she rereads a word she has read before, or she skips a word, or she shifts up or down a line, because the left eye is not picking up where the right eye stopped. The child is unaware that her eyes are doing this; she only knows that she keeps losing her place, no matter how hard she tries. Parents and teachers tell her to "Concentrate!" but that doesn't seem to solve the problem.

She may learn to compensate for the problem by reading with only one eye, perhaps by leaning her head on one hand as she reads, with that hand covering one eye. It is more likely that she will deal with the problem by avoiding reading whenever she can, because reading is difficult and frustrating, and actually gives her a headache.

What the good teacher will do to help: A good teacher who recognizes any kind of learning difficulty will recommend testing, and will also adapt the classroom to help the struggling child. For visual problems, the teacher should seat the child near the action and ensure adequate lighting. It sounds terribly old-fashioned, but it helps to require the child to sit up straight and hold his book at the proper angle. The teacher should encourage the use of large-print books (available in most libraries). The good teacher recognizes that some children learn best through their eyes, some through their ears, and some through their fingers, and will try to teach using all those modes so that all can learn. A sensitive teacher recognizes that a child with visual problems is quickly fatigued by reading and other intensely visual tasks.

HEARING AND SPEECH

Hearing: A child's hearing and speech develop with mechanisms much more complicated than the most expensive sound system. As with any complicated system, there are many different ways for the system to break down. It's not always obvious when a learning problem is a speech or hearing problem. Even when it's obvious that something is wrong, it's not always easy to pinpoint the location of the problem.

Symptoms: In measuring a child's vision, we do a lot more than differentiate between the blind and the not blind. We recognize many types and gradations of vision problems. In hearing, however, we seem to ignore any middle area between deaf and not deaf. But there are several aspects of hearing that should be considered.

Some children have perfect hearing over most of the range of sounds, but have limited hearing within some part of the range. They may be able to hear guttural sounds (G, K, X) better than sibilant sounds (S, C, Z) or vice versa.

Some children are able to pick out certain sounds from within a whole babble of sounds; others are confused by any distracting sounds.

Some children have a "microphone ear"; it cannot concentrate on a teacher's words because all the background noises call equally for his attention. With this phenomenon, the ear hears everything without selectivity, just as a microphone hears. Children with a "microphone ear" do better in a quiet classroom with few distractions. At home, they should study in a quiet place with no music or TV; they might even use earplugs.

Some children hear better during a particular part of the year. Hay fever season, or allergies of any kind, might decrease their hearing ability. Illnesses of various kinds can impair their hearing, either temporarily or permanently.

Children hear better when their ears are clean. Too much ear wax or other obstructions can decrease hearing. Children who clean their ears with pencil erasers may be sending a signal for help in this area.

In the classroom: Some children have more acute hearing than others. They can hear softer voices from greater distances. Seating them in the back of the classroom does not create a problem for them. At the other end of the scale, a child with poor hearing is really isolated if he's placed in the back of the classroom.

Some children hear better with one ear than the other. They need to be seated on a particular side of the classroom, with their good ear toward the teacher.

Some children can hear loud noises and soft noises, but they can't make the finer distinctions between similar sounds. They can't hear the differences between F and TH, between M and N, between W and WH, and so on. Some children can easily distinguish the consonant sounds, but are unable to sense the differences between similar vowel sounds.

Some children can tell the difference between sounds, but can't relate them to the appropriate letter symbols.

Speech: A child learns a new word by hearing it and then saying it. He tries hard to pronounce the new word exactly the way he heard it. That's why little Texans sound like big Texans and little Bostonians sound like big Bostonians. The child might not pronounce a word correctly on his first try, but he can usually get it right after a few attempts.

Symptoms: When a child cannot get it right, even after several tries, parents should consider some reasons why. If she is young enough to have all her baby teeth, perhaps she has not learned how to use lip and tongue muscles to make a particular sound—for example, the R sound.

If she has a full repertoire of alphabet sounds but cannot pronounce a specific word, it could mean that she is having trouble hearing the word or a part of the word. If she can't hear it properly, then she can't say it properly because she doesn't know what it should sound like. Or it could mean that she hears it, but is confusing the order of syllables or has some other perceptual problem. Perhaps she has trouble distinguishing vowel sounds, either in hearing them or saying them; perhaps she has trouble connecting a specific vowel sound that she hears, with the same vowel sound that she speaks. For adults, that connection is automatic. For a child, it's not always easier said than done.

In the classroom: Spelling is another indicator of possible hearing or auditory perception problems. Letter reversals may not point to auditory problems, but letter omissions might. Bizarre spelling might point to perceptual problems. If a child's spelling shows no evidence of using the phonics that he has been taught, perceptual problems may be the key. Or poor phonics training itself might be the key.

What the good teacher will do to help: Poor hearing inhibits learning, but a good teacher can minimize that problem. She can seat the child in front, or at her left or right. She can make sure she has the child's attention before giving instructions; she can put assignments on the board as well as announcing them; she can use a buddy system, appointing a classmate to make sure the instructions are received and understood; she can record instructions and assignments, possibly on voice mail so parents can access them.

ATTENTION

As you read at this moment, several things are happening. Your eyes and your brain are working together to give meaning to these printed symbols. Your eyes are concentrating on the written words, in a sequence running across the page from left to right. Within your field of vision, in addition to this book, is your desk or your lap. There are thousands of distracting objects within your field of vision, but you are ignoring them. Your eyes concentrate on the printed symbols and send messages to the brain: "This is what I see." Your brain has a kind of filtering system to eliminate distracting elements and allow you to concentrate on the "important" inputs. But some children have a breakdown in their filtering systems. A complete absence of filters is known as autism, while a weakness in the filtering system is a characteristic of attention deficit disorder (ADD).

Symptoms: ADD is often confused with hyperactivity because many children with one of these conditions also have the other. But it doesn't always happen that way; many lively children (80 percent of ADD cases are boys) have no attention deficits, and many ADD children do not have hyperactivity. The real identifying characteristics of ADD are distractibility (as mentioned above, the inability to filter inputs) and impulsivity, the inability to suppress responses.

In the classroom: Good teachers have always been able to deal with active children by simply channeling their energy into something productive. But when the activity is complicated by distractibility and impulsivity, it disrupts the classroom. Normal children bump into each other and tumble around like puppy dogs, but when an ADD child is bumped, he feels threatened and may lash out impulsively. The ADD child has no "off" switch, can't wait his turn, and needs constant supervision to prevent those eruptions.

What the good teacher will do to help: A bad teacher wants to give Ritalin to every lively child, just to make her teaching job easier. A good teacher knows the difference between ADD and hyperactivity, and can recommend ADD testing when appropriate. The good teacher will be patient and will create a calm, structured classroom environment; will reinforce appropriate behavior; and will control inappropriate behavior with time-outs rather than punishment. A good teacher tries very hard to teach the children to be less impulsive, and to show them how actions have consequences.

Processing Problems

VISUAL PERCEPTION

The eye is like a camera. It makes no sense of what it sees, and cannot choose what it will see or not see. When the eye sees an eight-sided figure, the brain is the part that counts the sides and labels it an octagon. If it is a red eight-sided figure, the brain provides the label "stop sign." The brain is constantly helping us organize and interpret the pastiche of colors, shapes, and sizes that is our vision. This process is called *perception*, and it plays a major role in learning. Sometimes a child has excellent vision and an excellent brain, but the teamwork between them is poor; we call this a visual perception problem. Eighty percent of the children with visual perception problems are boys.

Symptoms: Jimmy gets confused about what letter follows what. He tends to confuse *d* with *b*, *b* with *p*, and *g* with *q*. He often misspells and mispronounces because he has reversed the order of the letters. He can do addition better than subtraction. If the problem persists into third or fourth grade, he will be better at multiplication than division. Jimmy can draw pictures, but he finds it hard to copy pictures. He can't find Waldo anywhere. Looking at the night sky, he can't pick out the constellations.

In the classroom: All children in primary grades occasionally reverse letters and words. A few errors of this type should not send panicked parents scurrying for professional help, as the errors are a normal part of the child's development. If the errors are excessive, or if they persist beyond second grade, then some help might be in order.

Most mild visual perception problems simply disappear at about the age of nine, although serious problems can continue into adulthood. On the other hand, the nine-year-old who no longer has a visual perception problem is not completely out of the woods. He still has to deal with residual effects of the old problem, and so does his teacher.

What the good teacher will do to help: First, there was an awful lot of learning that Jimmy missed while he had the problem. He's got a lot of catching up to do, so he'll have to work twice as hard. And the teacher may have no desire to review all the stuff that Jimmy missed; in fact, the teacher may not be aware of Jimmy's need to review all the content of the primary grades.

Second, Jimmy had the perceptual problem for years, and the problem colored his attitudes throughout that time. He came to think of reading as punishment; he came to think of effort as fruitless; and he came to think of himself as stupid and helpless. He may have outgrown the basic problem, but he still has to deal with the attitudes that it created. A sympathetic teacher will recognize the situation and give Jimmy lots of encouragement and positive reinforcement.

MEMORY

A century ago, education consisted largely of memory training. Children were required to memorize the alphabet sounds, addition facts, and the multiplication tables, just as they are today. They were also required to memorize poems, speeches, Bible verses, classical literature, royal chronologies, presidents, facts about the states, and so on.

Symptoms: There are many different kinds of memories. Poor auditory memory may show up in the inability to remember the words to popular songs or friends' telephone numbers. Poor kinesthetic memory shows up in the inability to remember sequences of dance steps or the mechanics of the serve in tennis. Poor visual memory may show itself in slow learning of vocabulary.

In the classroom: Children today are asked to understand more and memorize less. This is generally an improvement in educational methodology, but with one negative side effect: Children who don't practice memorization skills will be less skilled at memorization. More children today struggle with those fundamentals that must be memorized—the addition facts and the multiplication tables. To some extent, vocabulary is memorized, so the child with poor memory skills may have a limited vocabulary, resulting in lower reading ability. Furthermore, research has established that thought and language are strongly related; a limited vocabulary limits thinking ability and a more extensive vocabulary enables more precise thinking processes.

What the good teacher will do to help: A good teacher will assign enough interesting memory work to help children improve their memorization skills. In addition, the good teacher will do things to help children who now have poor skills: use repetition and review, provide mnemonics, use singing and rhyme, teach outlining skills. Some recent research indicates that classical music in the background improves memorization ability. Other research points out the obvious—that it is easier to memorize things you find interesting; so teachers need to make even the memory work seem interesting.

Output Problems

MOTOR

When a child has a physical disability, it is usually quite obvious to parents and teachers alike. Most states have laws protecting the rights of disabled children, and most school districts have made provisions to help such children. For most serious physical problems, the symptoms are obvious and well defined by research and in the law. But what if the physical problem is not so obvious? What if the child has symptoms that don't quite qualify him as legally disabled? Does that mean he has no problem at all?

Symptoms: A child who is clumsy and uncoordinated has a problem that is very real to him. Because he is not a deep metaphysical thinker who can separate his corporeal body from his essential self, his body and his soul are one thing to him. When he trips over a sidewalk crack, he thinks of himself as stupid.

When teams are picked for dodgeball and he is chosen last, he doesn't say to himself, "Well, my coordination is poor, but I have compensating virtues." Instead he thinks, "I'm worthless and nobody likes me. My classmates think I'm the worst at everything."

When the teacher criticizes his work for messiness, he can't explain that his thoughts are orderly and well structured, but the fingers can't seem to get it down neatly on paper. He accepts the teacher's implied judgment that he is sloppy and disorganized.

In the classroom: When his classmates laugh at him for his clumsiness, he is sure that he is worthless and stupid. He might react by giving up, or becoming the class clown, or being angry and disruptive; whatever the reaction, it will probably hinder his learning.

Problems with small-muscle coordination may not appear as obvious to a parent, but teachers are very aware of them. The small muscles are used for holding pencils and scissors, drawing and writing. In the primary grades, poor small-muscle coordination gets recognition as a problem, and some help, from sympathetic teachers. If the child gets beyond the primary grades without solving the problem, the sympathy often disappears. The child is labeled "lazy," "careless," "sloppy," and "disorganized."

What the good teacher can do to help: A good school has a physical education program that is more than just recess with a coach. In the elementary grades, the PE program should be more concerned with development of coordination than with team sports. A good teacher will recognize a child's motor problem and will be sympathetic to all the ramifications of the basic problem. In the classroom, the teacher might allow more time on written tests, encourage use of a word processor, place less importance on handwriting, and refer children for testing and remedial training.

TO TEST OR NOT TO TEST

As parents, if you think your child may have a serious learning problem, you should definitely request an evaluation by your local public school. School districts are required by the Individuals with Disabilities Education Act (PL 94-192 of 1975, known as IDEA) to act upon your *written* request. If your child does not have an obvious handicap but might be classified as hyperactive, dyslexic, or having attention deficit disorder, you can request evaluation under Section 504 of the Rehabilitation Act of 1973, and the local school is required to respond to your written request within fifteen days, with a plan for assessing your child's needs. They must give you some indication about which tests will be used, and they must get your permission to give the tests. Then they must come up with an Individual Education Plan (IEP) for your child within fifty days. The IEP includes the child's current level of performance, services to be provided either in the classroom or elsewhere in the school, related services available (therapy, transportation, and so on), and the amount of time to be spent in a regular classroom, among other details.

You may ask whether you want your child to enter the world of special education. There is the danger that she might label herself as inferior, and then lower her aspirations to match her low self-esteem. And there is the likelihood that other children will label her inferior; children are rarely cruel by intention, but are often cruel by insensitivity. However, if your child needs the extra help, you should get it for her.

You can limit the extent to which your child is sucked into the special education vortex. At each step in the IEP process, you can stop the school from excessive zeal in pushing your child into special ed. You can restrict the kinds of testing they give her. You can have your own testing done (sometimes at their expense). You can reject part or all of the IEP. You can reject any plan that takes her out of the regular classroom. There are lots of safeguards for parents built into the law.

And like so much legislation, IDEA and Section 504 of the Rehabilitation Act were written with a complete disregard for cost. Whenever the federal government takes responsibility, cost controls go out the window. The federal government passed the laws stating that if your child needs services, then she *must* be provided with services by her local school district, but they haven't provided sufficient federal funding to pay for the mandated services. Nevertheless, *lack of funding is not a valid excuse* for the district to refuse service to your child. Some school districts solve the funding problem by exploiting Section 504, diagnosing half their students as hyperactive or ADD in order to get more federal funding.

REASSURING YOUR CHILD

School is the center of a child's intellectual and social life. Performing poorly in school is devastating to a child. This is especially true if the child has no idea why he is doing poorly, or if the remedial plan that he believed would help him doesn't seem to be helping at all. The child will need a lot of reassurance, support, and unconditional love from his parents.

Sympathetic parents want to make boo-boos go away. They want to give the little guy a hug and say, "There, there, it's going to be all right. Mommy and Daddy will take care of it." But there are several things wrong with this approach. In the first place, it's possible that Mommy and Daddy haven't the knowledge, the time, or the power needed to solve the problem. Second, this approach sends the message that solving the problem is out of the child's hands, and that the child shouldn't even bother to try to help himself. And third, solving the problem may be your goal, but it isn't the child's. The child simply wants the problem to go away so he can feel just like everybody else. He does not want to be the object of a fuss, set apart from his peers, or thought of as a student requiring special treatment. He doesn't want himself to be thought of as different or deficient in any way. So when the well-intentioned parent talks about "solving his problem," the child sees it as recognition that he has a problem or, worse, that he *is* a problem.

Children—like adults and flies—are attracted more by honey than by vinegar. For that reason, you should always focus on what the child is doing well, and keep the praise flowing. If you can't praise the child's accomplishments, praise her attitude and her persistence. Don't harp on the problem; emphasize the child's efforts to overcome the problem. Make sure you are there to guide and support her. And always talk in terms of working together, instead of exhorting the child to do better on her own (she needs to know that you are on her team). If the child will be subjected to further testing or an evaluation, she should be reassured that the testing is to find out how parents and teachers can do a better job of helping her to learn. Minimize the idea that the testing is to find out what is *wrong* with her.

While it can be very tempting for parents to reassure the child by saying that the problem is the teacher's fault, this is rarely a productive approach . . . even when it is true. Until all of the evidence is in, there is always the possibility that you are wrong, that the teacher is not at fault.

But even if the teacher is to blame, assigning blame does not solve the problem—it may even create one. Keep your focus on the main goal, which is to improve the quality of your child's education. Telling him that his teacher is incompetent, *even if it is true,* adds nothing to his educational experience. And because destroying the child's faith in this teacher might also destroy his faith in teaching in general, such an approach may damage his interactions with all future teachers, undermine his joy of learning, and have a negative effect on his education for years to come.

So you can't tell your child that his teacher is to blame.

But, when the time is right, you can say it directly to the teacher. In the next section of this book, you will learn how to confront the bad teacher, advocate effectively on behalf of your child, and use all available tools to end your child's misery before his self-esteem and intellectual curiosity are eroded. Will your child thank you for your efforts? Probably not. But he's counting on you nonetheless.

PART TWO

SAVING

YOUR

CHILD

6

Bad Teachers: Who They Are

The lawns are still lush and green, but the trees are beginning to drop their leaves in showers of gold and red. The leaves swirl as the children race their bicycles through them on the way to soccer practice. Life is good here, safe and happy. The families here share the same values, priorities, and ambitions for their children. Many families moved here because of the good school system, some of them sacrificing their life savings and mortgaging their future earnings to make the move. Others have lived and paid school taxes here for many years. All of them have invested something—their lives or their money—in the community.

Some of the parents in this typical American community send their children to private schools. They believe that, although the public schools are well regarded, a private education is a better education. Some parents believe the public schools do a fine job and they refuse to consider private schools. In either case, the parents have made the best choice for their child according to their values, and they will defend that choice.

The educational choices you make for your child are intensely personal because they directly express your lifestyle and values. If you are like most middle-income parents, you have sacrificed opportunities for greater income, or for alternative ways to spend that income, so that you could live in this neighborhood and send your children to this school. You want to believe that you have made the right choices.

Also like many parents, you may have nagging doubts about the school, because you feel that the children aren't learning. More to the point, you feel your own child isn't learning. You don't want to believe that it's the school's fault, because to question the quality of the school is to question your decision to live in this neighborhood; and the alternatives to that scenario are too awful to think about. Having invested your lives and money in this school, you don't want to face the possibility that you aren't getting a payoff.

Perhaps the neighborhood is great, the school is great, but your child's teacher is bad. Can that be? Can a good school system have bad teachers? The truth is that bad teachers can be found anywhere, even in excellent school districts. The school administrators won't tell you who they are—they themselves may not even know; their definition of "bad" is different from yours.

Who Is Qualified to Judge a Teacher? You Are!

What is a good teacher? Who has the right to decide what a good teacher is? Who has the right to certify that someone is a good teacher? There are long arguments over these questions among school districts, teacher unions, teacher colleges, and others; but the solution can be seen in this simple analogy.

What is a good car wash? Is it the one certified by the American Society of Car Washes? Is it the one endorsed by the Chamber of Commerce? No. It's the one that people keep going to, because it does a good job of cleaning cars. It may not have any fancy certificates on the wall, but it's the one that meets the people's needs.

Teaching is a service industry, too. And the bottom line is that the best teacher is the one who meets the needs of the consumer by getting the most out of the students. If a teacher has fancy certificates and glowing recommendations from the principal but can't help his students to achieve, then that's a bad teacher. A teacher without certificates who antagonizes his principal but gets children to achieve is a good teacher.

In fact, in many schools the principal has no idea who the good teachers are. Certainly, the principal *should* know which teachers are causing the most learning, and which are causing the least. And one would expect that the principals' ratings of teachers would be based on how much learning they caused, but that is not the case. When administrators rate the quality of teachers, evidence shows that the ratings have no relation to student learning. In fact, the higher the rating given by an administrator, the less likely it is that the teacher gets good results in terms of student achievement.[1]

Nor are fellow teachers any better at identifying effective teachers. When asked to rate their peers, their ratings also show no connection to student learning. Apparently, many teachers don't know good teaching when they see it.

The only people in the educational arena who can distinguish a good teacher from a bad one are the students themselves and their parents. When teachers are rated by parents or students, those ratings show a definite relationship to student achievement; the higher the teacher's rating, the higher the achievement of her students. As common sense would dictate, the customer is always right. The customer knows when the service is good or bad. The customer isn't fooled by phony certificates or endorsements; results are what counts.

That's why I suggest to parents, particularly those whose children are beginning a new year with a new teacher, to get opinions from the parents whose children have been in that classroom. They may not know whether their teacher has filed all her paperwork on time (the principal would know that), or whether she is popular in the teachers' lounge (her colleagues would know that), but parents will know whether their child has been happy, inspired, terrorized, comforted, or belittled in that classroom. And, on the whole, their opinion will be more accurate and better informed than the principal's or the other teachers' opinions.

My next suggestion to concerned parents is that they trust their own instincts about the teacher. That is not always easy. Parents have been led to believe that American schools are like the Emerald City, where magical things can happen to transform our children into more perfect beings. Parents are also instructed, "Don't look behind that curtain!" In other words, don't ask whether the educators are real wizards or only masters of illusion. Don't question the experts' judgment in matters of which you know nothing. Since parents are not "trained educators," the assumption is that they are not qualified to judge a teacher's performance. As the school year moves along, you may or may not learn a lot about the teacher. But you will certainly learn a lot about the teacher's impact on your child.

And that, of course, is what education is all about: not about the teacher's performance on Parents' Night or in an administrator's eyes, but about the teacher's ability to get the *children* to perform on a daily basis.

What Is a Bad Teacher?

Parents are aware of numerous ways that teachers can be incompetent, some of which are not even recognized by school administrators. Because schools have fuzzy ideas about what contributes to teacher quality, schools may have very high opinions of some very incompetent teachers. From a parent's point of view, here are some types of teachers who are not competent to teach children:

- Teachers who lack knowledge of the subject matter
- Teachers with poor classroom control
- Teachers who behave unprofessionally
- Teachers who can't diagnose learning problems
- Teachers who are obsessive about method
- Teachers who focus on the wrong goals
- Teachers who have no goals at all

Very few of these teachers need to worry about being fired, because very few of these conditions are grounds for dismissal from a school district. But each of these teachers creates a miserable learning environment for a child, and a host of problems in the classroom and beyond.

LACK OF KNOWLEDGE OF THE SUBJECT MATTER

Is it a disastrous problem when a teacher is not very intelligent? Not really. The elementary school teacher is not expected to explain the minutiae of foreign policy or the economic factors influencing the semiconductor market. Qualities other than intelligence are more critical to successful classroom teaching.

But at any grade level, it is absolutely necessary for the teacher to understand the subject he is teaching. He cannot teach arithmetic if he can't add. He can't teach reading if he is barely literate. He can't teach children to write if he can't write properly himself.

Why do schools hire people who can't even read, write, or compute at the eighth-grade level? (And how did they ever get their college degrees? That's another tale.) Some were hired to teach athletics, or supervise playgrounds, or because their uncle happened to be a school superintendent, and then they were transferred to classroom duty. But most of them were hired directly as classroom teachers of children, and most of them were hired with full knowledge of their lack of basic skills. Several studies in different states and school districts give the same results: about one-third of the teachers fail an eighth-grade test of basic skills.

Clearly, no substandard teacher is eager to submit to testing that will expose her ignorance of basic skills. She pays union dues to support lobbyists at the state capital; those lobbyists' main function is to protect her from competency testing. So in most states, there is no measure of teacher competence in basic skills.

Still, parents should wonder if the teachers of their children are qualified. They will have to look for telltale clues in more subtle ways. Here are a few things to look for:

1. The absence of notices from the teacher about class activities. Many good teachers try to keep parents informed about what goes on in class. If there are no notices, it could mean that the teacher is a poor writer.

2. Notes from the teacher that contain misspelled words and grammatical errors; this isn't just a clue, this is plain evidence that the teacher lacks fundamental skills.

3. The absence of graded papers, especially compositions. If the child is never asked to write, it may be because the teacher hasn't the skills to correct written work. If the child is asked to write, *some* compositions will not be corrected, because a good teacher wants children to write with fluency and expressiveness. But if the compositions are *never* corrected by the teacher, it may indicate the teacher's lack of skills.

4. Missing subjects. If the teacher is very poor in a particular subject, she is likely to avoid it and concentrate instead on things she knows better. If the teacher never spends time on art, or music, or science, then that's unfortunate for the child, but not devastating. On the other hand, if the teacher skims over arithmetic, or reading, or writing, then the child is being cheated out of something essential to his future.

POOR CLASSROOM CONTROL

The principal sits in his office dreaming of retirement, until his reverie is disturbed by noises from Miss Livesey's class down the hall. His first reaction is to chastise Miss Livesey. Her children are disorderly, she can't control her students, and therefore she is a bad teacher. As usual, the principal is wrong. Principals are very poor judges of teacher quality, particularly when it comes to the issue of classroom control. Many principals prize quiet classrooms that don't disturb other classrooms. They expect teachers to maintain quiet classrooms, and they judge teachers more on the ability to maintain quiet than on their ability to teach.

The happy truth is that teachers can be in perfect control of a noisy room if all the children are busily working on educational projects. Enthusiasm is an essential part of education. Alternatively, silence in a classroom does not always signify that learning is going on. It may simply show that teacher and students alike have no enthusiasm for the learning process.

We should remember, though, that sometimes a disorderly classroom may be just exactly what it appears to be. If the children are not focused on educational tasks set by the teacher, then not much learning is going on. It may be that the teacher is doing a bad job of teaching, based on a bad job of planning, and compounded by bad skills in managing and motivating children. This is a bad teacher.

Children learn more in a subject if they spend more time on it. This factor, known as "time on task," explains a lot about learning. It explains why Japanese children achieve more than American children; they simply spend more time on academics, both in class time and homework time. Time on task also explains why children who read at home are better students than those who don't.

The quality of a teacher's classroom control, then, has a huge effect on a child's education, because classroom control impacts time on task. In the room of a teacher with poor control, not enough time is spent on academics because too much time must be spent on discipline. Another child's misbehavior affects your child's learning, because it draws your child's time and attention away from her work.

In recent years, children who belong in special education classes because of physical, mental, or psychological handicaps have been "mainstreamed" into regular classrooms. This practice, while beneficial to handicapped children, has placed great stress on teachers' ability to maintain classroom control, and decreases time on task for other children in the classroom.

What can parents look for, in terms of appropriate classroom control and time on task?

1. Look in on the classroom, as much as school rules allow. Don't draw conclusions from observations on parent visiting days, as these are not representative of a typical day. And don't draw conclusions from observing the last minutes of a school day, as these are universally chaotic.

2. While observing, don't compare the class to the Victorian model of a teacher lecturing to a silent room with orderly rows of desks. Remember that enthusiasm is a good thing.

3. Observe the transitional periods. When the class shifts from one subject to another, how long does it take the class to shift focus? Some teachers lose as much as 10 percent of their time on task during transitions.

4. Measure results. Talk to your child about how much work is being done in class. Ask whether other students are interfering with his working.

5. Ask about school policies on "mainstreaming" spe-

cial education students into regular classrooms, and what it takes to reverse a decision to mainstream an especially destructive child.

UNPROFESSIONAL CONDUCT

Teachers can be disciplined or even fired for "unprofessional conduct." Parents may welcome that information, thinking that such a policy may keep unprofessional or amateurish teachers out of the classroom, but that is not the case. "Unprofessional conduct" is defined by school administrators, not parents. Since administrators care more about the smooth operation of the school than about the learning that goes on inside the school, it is logical that "unprofessional conduct" is conduct that interferes with management, not conduct that interferes with learning. In the school, nobody places much importance on learning.

Unprofessional conduct, as defined by school administrators and their lawyers, includes such things as:

- improper attire
- poor attitude toward administrators
- not turning in attendance reports or lesson plans
- neglect of duty (usually, leaving children unsupervised)

Unprofessional conduct may also include excessive absenteeism, but only if the absenteeism is deliberate and willful. If the absenteeism is due to health problems, which (according to the law) include alcoholism and drug abuse, it is not considered unprofessional conduct and will probably not lead to termination.

Notice that there is nothing in the legal definition of

"unprofessional conduct" that describes the teacher's relation to the *students*. A teacher can be appallingly amateurish in the classroom, or abusive, or indifferent, without qualifying as unprofessional. It is only when the teacher offends the administration that he or she becomes unprofessional. In this area, it is difficult for parents to target "unprofessionalism" since only the administration can declare a teacher as "unprofessional." So, what symptoms should the parents look for? Don't even bother to look.

TEACHERS WHO CAN'T DIAGNOSE LEARNING PROBLEMS

A child is an enormously complex creature, a romping laboratory of billions of cells and electrical impulses. The child's mind and body are constantly inventing and copying new motions and thought. Most parts of the mind and body work pretty well together, most of the time; in any child, some parts work better than others. And in some children, some parts don't work at all.

The parts that don't work well have a major effect on learning. A child could have 20/20 vision and still have a vision problem when he reads. A child could have perfect hearing, except for a certain high note. A child could have an excellent memory of last year, but not of the last hour. A child could be a great athlete who can't write the alphabet. Every child is different, and every difference has educational consequences.

A good teacher should recognize that some children learn by listening, some by seeing, and some by feeling; and his classroom surely contains children with each learning style. The teacher should recognize that some children are facile with words, some with numbers, and some with neither; and that children vary widely in the amount of time needed to absorb knowledge. Most of all, an adequate teacher must realize that, if a child is doing badly in school, there is always a reason; and the reason is rarely laziness or willfulness. The child who is doing the very best she can and has no idea why she is not succeeding is depending on the teacher to find out why her struggles are in vain. If the teacher can't figure it out, then the child is in store for years of frustration.

What can parents do? Ask very specific questions during parent conferences, as discussed in Chapters 2 and 3. Also, parents might share information about children with learning problems, noting which teachers had taught those children without detecting the problems.

TEACHERS OBSESSED WITH METHOD

Learning is a mysterious process that happens inside a child's head. Teaching is a mystifying process that comes out of a teacher's mouth. In the best of all worlds, teaching leads to solid learning, but in the real world, the connection between teaching and learning is often obscure. In a good teacher's classroom, for example, social studies teaching may be going on and the children are learning social studies. In the method-obsessed teacher's classroom, on the other hand, there is also social studies teaching going on, but the children are not learning social studies. Their minds are far from the classroom, in far-flung fields and playgrounds, and they are wondering why teachers are so unimaginative, unfair, and unkind. It is no wonder so many children loathe school.

In her defense—though it's a weak defense—the teacher can't help it. She is doing what she was trained to do, and what her boss wants her to do. Her teacher training classes focused on methodology. In her How to Teach Arithmetic course, she was taught that if she follows the approved method, she will be an approved teacher. She was also taught that the approved method leads to student learning and that the accepted method is the *only* path to student learning. In teacher training, no one ever questions these assumptions. The training method equals student learning as clearly as two plus two equals four.

The school principal has no way of knowing whether student learning is going on, because he can't see inside the children's heads. He could look at his pupils' once-a-year standardized achievement test scores, but he doesn't trust the tests' validity because the scores are too low. So he, too, does what *he* was trained to do—he assumes that approved teaching methodology equals student learning. He goes into the classroom and looks not for evidence of student learning but for evidence of approved teaching methodology. In our schools, style has triumphed over substance.

This is very sad for our schools, because approved teaching methodology does not equal student learning, and there are many reasons. The biggest reason is that approved teaching methodology is not even aimed at student learning; its goal is classroom management, which is a whole lot different from learning.

Learning occurs best when you have a child sitting at one end of a log and a great teacher sitting at the other end. Education in America drifts far from this ideal because, economically, we can't afford a 1:1 pupil-teacher ratio. We can grumblingly afford a 20:1 ratio, but teaching twenty kids is quite different from teaching only one.

Having twenty (or more) children in one classroom, with
wide differences in abilities and attitudes, requires that a
teacher have skills in organizing and supervising children
before any learning begins.

Teacher training recognizes this very real problem,
and gives teachers the skills they will need to organize
and manage a classroom full of children. The problems
arise because the best way to manage is not the best way
to educate, but given a choice between the two, principals and teachers prefer to manage rather than to educate.

Parents should be concerned if their child's teacher is
enamored of approved teaching methodology. Here are
some of the things parents can do:

1. Beware of new teachers fresh from college and recently certified. They have been indoctrinated in the approved methodology, and haven't enough experience to
question what the "experts" have taught them.

2. Listen to the teacher talk. If she talks about what
she is doing rather than on what the children are doing,
gently bring the focus back to the children. Ask how the
teacher knows whether the methods are working; ask for
evidence that the children are learning.

3. Ask the teacher's opinion of Madeline Hunter. If
you are lucky, you will get a blank stare. If you are un-
lucky, the teacher will light up with praise of the Hunter
approach. Madeline Hunter is the high priestess of a
movement that raises methodology to a religion. She has
developed a structured, systematic approach to teaching
that appears to be very scientific. Her approach has been
adopted by school districts in many states.

The Hunter method reduces teaching to a list of steps

so simple that even the dullest teacher can follow them, so it appeals to a wide audience. It helps teachers run those quiet classrooms that are so prized by principals, and it minimizes behavior problems (unless you consider stupor to be a behavior problem). The Hunter method has given the delusion of competence to thousands of mediocre teachers.

What it has not done, unfortunately, is increase student learning. In all the schools and systems where it has been employed, the Hunter method has failed to increase student learning. Consistently in all of those schools, administrators expect that increases in achievement will "show up soon"; but the improvement never appears. The same administrators who could never tell the difference between learning and classroom management will forever be waiting in vain for improved classroom management to equal improved learning.

TEACHERS WHO FOCUS ON GOALS
OTHER THAN EDUCATION

No one really cares whether your child learns anything at school. The principal and each teacher at your child's school has other priorities that are more important to them; often these goals include political, social, psychological, and multicultural goals. The education of one child is just not a high-priority item—except to the parents of that one child.

You think it's not possible that your school has so little concern for your child's education? Consider this: Researchers from UCLA listed 145 possible goals for elementary education, then asked teachers to rank them in order of importance. The teachers' top 8 goals, out of 145, were:

1. Self-esteem
2. Attitude toward school
3. Need achievement
4. Socialization
5. Friendliness
6. Independence
7. Listening reaction and response
8. Sportsmanship

Now, all of these are creditable goals. Ultimately—that is, by the time a child reaches adulthood—education has little to do with accumulating facts and everything to do with building character. Perhaps we should be glad that schoolteachers recognize this. But what ever happened to reading, writing, and arithmetic? Don't they deserve a place *somewhere* in the top eight?

We want our children to be happy, well-adjusted people. And we want our schools to help them become happy and well adjusted. But we must raise our eyebrows just a little when the teachers' top goals are *all* behavioral. We wonder whether the teachers' priority ranking acknowledges the ultimate importance of character building, or does it say that teachers are most interested in the things that make for a serene classroom? Maybe it doesn't really matter to the teacher whether anyone learns anything, so long as no child makes the day unpleasant.

Any teacher will tell you that she cares about your child, and she does. She also cares about recycling, nuclear war, and the homeless. But all of these concerns, including any concerns she may have for your child, take a lower priority than her concern about her time, her income, the other children, her professional reputation, her boss's opinion of her, her coworkers' opinions of her, her emotional needs, and her serenity. If she insists that she really does care about your child, politely suggest some ways she could put caring into practice—specifically, devoting time and effort to your individual child. Then you will see exactly where your child's education falls among her priorities.

And what about the principal? Surely your child's achievement is important to him. Maybe . . . maybe not. Many school principals will happily sell your child down the river for any of several reasons. He has to defend his teachers, even when they are wrong, in order to maintain his rapport with the staff. He has to defend school district policies, even when they are wrong, in order to maintain his standing with school district headquarters. He has to defend his own decisions and policies, even when they are wrong, in order to maintain the illusion of leadership. None of that leaves much time for defending your child's right to a quality education.

School principals were asked to rate the same 145 goals of elementary education, and their ratings were almost identical to the teachers' ratings. In other words, like the teachers, they don't care where the ship goes, as long as it avoids rough weather. Principals have a set of priorities that are more important to them than your child's education.

An organization that values its own internal rules more than it values its clients—that's the definition of a bureaucracy. And a school system, with its rigid, self-serving internal policies, is a classic bureaucracy. School personnel are just agents of the bureaucracy, blindly committed to following district policies without regard to the needs of an individual child. There is no point in being angry with the teacher or the principal for being what they are; just don't expect very much from them. They think that because it is school district policy to treat all parents like dirt, you must be dirt, too.

It is significant to note that parents, when asked to rate the same 145 goals, rated reading, writing, and arithmetic much higher than the teachers or principals did. As ever, the customer is always right. What can parents do, then, to find teachers who value basic skills?

1. Find teachers who believe in standardized tests and are willing to be held accountable for the classes' scores.
2. Find teachers who enthusiastically encourage outside reading.
3. Find teachers who can actually state their goals for the year, and state them in terms of measurable results.

TEACHERS WITH NO GOALS AT ALL

If your goal is to go to Atlanta, it helps to *know* that you want to go to Atlanta. Then, it helps to know where Atlanta is. If you don't know where you want to go, you might end up in Atlanta, but don't bet a year of your life on it.

Teachers should start every school year by considering their goals. What do I want my students to become? What kind of people should they be at the end of the year? What skills and abilities should they have by the end of the year? What do I have to do to get them there?

Rarely do teachers actually go through this process. Usually they assume that their textbooks will determine the goals and objectives for the year; and that if they get through the textbooks during the school year, they will have achieved their goals. And they will be wrong. There are several big reasons why a textbook's objectives are not the same as a classroom's objectives.

Let's imagine a textbook publisher trying to help your child learn to play soccer. First, the textbook publisher will choose a committee to write a textbook for teaching the skills necessary to play the game. The committee will not agree on what the important skills are, so they will include all possible skills. Then, in order to keep the book short and simple, they won't give enough emphasis to the really crucial skills. However, they will include sections on the history of soccer and other background information—interesting perhaps, but not useful to the child on the field.

Then, because the publisher wants to sell to big school districts, all the examples and illustrations will feature players from California, Texas, and New York. Also because of market considerations, the language of the book will be simplified; that is, a book for fourth graders will be written so a second-grader can read it. Most textbooks are "dumbed down" two grade levels.

Any really helpful instruction, such as how to kick the ball, will be found not in the textbook itself but in the teacher's edition. The teacher may actually use the teacher's edition in the first year of introduction, but may never open it again afterwards. So most children will never benefit from the only useful part of the textbook series.

Textbook publishers recognize the low quality of many American teachers, so they try to "teacher-proof" the textbooks, making them so simple that even a teacher can use them. Of course, this results in books that are simpleminded pabulum, not interesting to anyone.

So a textbook is a book that doesn't stick to its topic, isn't effective on the topic, isn't written for your child's age, and is so full of holes that it requires a companion book (the teacher's edition) to do what the text is supposed to do. The textbook's goals are so diffuse and so diluted that they are not practical goals for the user, the student.

The teacher depends on these texts for direction, but she may not know what the textbooks' avowed goals *are*. And the children certainly don't know that there are goals. A teacher whose goal is to follow the textbook is a teacher with no goals at all. Consequently, the child finishes the year nowhere near Atlanta, and probably very close to where he started.

What can parents do? Ask! Early in the school year, ask the teacher what her goals are for the year. Listen for the awkward silence or for her intention to follow the textbook. Ask what practical, applicable skills and abilities the students should have acquired by the end of the year; and make sure the response describes skills and abilities, not lists of factual content taken from the introduction to the teacher's edition.

Why Are There So Many Bad Teachers?

If bad teachers are so easily identifiable to parents, how can they be so invisible to school administrators? Are they looking in the wrong places? Why don't the schools find them and get rid of them?

The best college students never chose teaching as a major or as a career.[2] Of those who chose teaching, the best ones never got hired.[3] Of those who were hired, the best ones left teaching early in their lives.[4] Of those who are still teaching, most don't care whether your child learns or not. So who is teaching your child? Is it a bright, enthusiastic motivator of young minds? Or is it a garden-variety bad teacher, a leftover on the educational smorgasbord?

Across the nation and across the years, teacher candidates score far below average on the SAT, the American College Test, the Graduate Record Exam, and the National Assessment of Educational Progress. Regardless of what measure is used, teacher candidates seem to be relatively incompetent.

Sadly, the picture does not improve when you look at the intelligence of teachers in the classroom. A study in Dallas found that half the teachers "fail" a test of simple logic.[5] A look at the hiring record of the Los Angeles school system shows that many of the newly hired teachers are almost literate . . . *almost*.

The CBEST test—which measures a teacher's mastery of basic math, reading, and grammar—is used by many school districts in hiring decisions. It is set at the eighth grade level; still, many prospective teachers fail. Of course, many of those who fail are hired anyway, but only on a provisional basis.

It's hard to believe, but the evidence also shows that school districts look at this pool of very weak candidates, and then hire the least capable ones in the pool! Incredibly, the brighter candidates are not offered jobs; the less intelligent ones are hired.[6]

Fully half of the people who become teachers leave the field within the first six years. Some of them leave to get married or have children; others leave when they realize they can never raise a family on a teacher's salary. A few leave because they acknowledge that they are lousy teachers, but that is rare. Most leave because, when they leave teaching, it's hard to find a job that pays less. An ambitious person wants to step up into trash collecting, or cesspool cleaning, or anything that offers more income and a better future than teaching. For whatever reason, the quality of those who stay in teaching is lower than those who leave for greener pastures.

Those who stay in teaching seem to be the worst of the very weak collection who started out as teachers. Perhaps they stayed because, for those individuals, job prospects outside teaching would be slim. Or perhaps these are the people who lack the initiative and courage to pick up and make a new start. Many of them regret staying; almost half of today's teachers would not go into teaching if they had their lives to live over again.

But they stay; and are they better teachers because they have stayed? Studies have shown that children do not learn more with experienced teachers. It may be true that some individual teachers do improve with experience; it may also be true that an individual teacher gets worse over the years as experience replaces enthusiasm. It may be that younger teachers get better results because they are more enthusiastic, or because they are (on average) smarter than the older ones. It may be that a teacher with twenty-three years' experience really only has one year's experience, repeated twenty-three times. Whatever the explanation, the research shows that teacher experience is not related to student achievement.

PHYSICAL AND PSYCHOLOGICAL FACTORS

In any group of a million people, there must be a wide range of differences. People will vary in height, weight, hair color, skin color, blood type, intelligence; there will be differences in every measurable attribute. There will be differences in physical health and fitness, as well as differences in every aspect of emotional and mental health.

A group of one million elementary school teachers will certainly reflect this wide range of differences. In terms of physical abilities, there will be some serious athletes, some weekend athletes, some armchair athletes. There will be the physically gifted and the physically handicapped, and everything in between; most of the one million are physically healthy enough to teach school. Some excellent teachers teach from wheelchairs, and some have guide dogs.

On the other hand, some teachers are made incompetent by health problems. A few of them are trying hard to overcome physical handicaps but simply cannot succeed. Children are sympathetic to problems, but they have short memories and can be thoughtlessly cruel. A child's sympathy is real, but his desire to play is just as real, and sometimes more pressing. With effort, a handicapped teacher may win control over her own unwilling body; but if she can't control her roomful of small bodies, she can't teach.

These observations may seem rather obvious, but they become more critical when we consider that not all of the variations that make teachers unique are physical ones. The group of a million teachers includes many wonderful ones, some crazy ones, some cruel ones, and some perverted ones. Any weirdness that can be found in the general population can be found among teachers, too. Consider the suburban teacher who saw a deer outside his classroom; he attacked and killed it with a hunting knife as his students watched, openmouthed. Or the teacher in a fundamentalist school who beat his students, to "drive the devil out of them." Or the teacher who molested children at five different schools; he was never arrested or even fired, just transferred to the next school.

Psychological problems affect people in all professions, but psychological problems in teachers affect children, too, in mysterious and subtle ways. Teachers don't wear signs that say, "I'm nuts!" or "I'm depressed today," so children have no warning. Nor do children, especially those in the primary grades, have well-developed mechanisms for identifying aberrant behavior in adults. In the classroom, children tend to adapt to the teacher's set norms. A teacher who yells, smacks a ruler against a desk, or sulks will upset her students, but children aren't apt to complain or object. They are more apt to "play sick" instead.

Teachers are expected to act like "professionals," which some interpret to mean "detached" and "dispassionate." Teachers feel a great restriction on their freedom to show emotions. They are trained and encouraged to deny and repress emotions like fear, hate, tenderness, joy, or compassion.[7] That sort of suppression of natural human emotions might be easier—and more realistic—if teachers weren't also laboring under a good deal of pressure from other sources.

"Other concerns expressed include the burden of conformity, under which many labor (in the name of being sensible and socially well-adjusted); the oppressive load imposed by striving to live up to an impossible ideal—a kind of striving some educators cultivate as though it were a virtue."[8]

Some teachers respond to all these pressures with a

vague hostility toward school, or their bosses, or the subject matter, or their career. Worst of all, a teacher might focus her anger on the children.

This might take the form of angry blowups or excessive reaction to minor annoyances, and the child who is the target of the anger might vary from day to day. Another form of teacher anger could be a lower-level hostility, over a longer period of time, directed at an entire class. The most pathological expression of teacher anger is hostility directed consistently at one child over a period of time.

WHY SCHOOLS REWARD BAD TEACHERS

By now you may be wondering whether teacher standards exist in this country and why those standards aren't working to weed the bad teachers out. The fact is, every state has teacher certification standards, along with colleges or courses to prepare students for this certification. Vast amounts of money and effort are expended by the state and by the teacher trainees for pieces of paper that signify nothing.

Teacher training might have some purpose if anyone could identify what makes a great teacher, and then try to mold teachers in that image. In the teacher training industry, everyone has an opinion about how to make better teachers, but no one can back up their opinion with facts. Very little research has ever been done; and the little research that exists has been systematically ignored.

So teacher colleges don't know what a good teacher is or how to produce one. School administrators don't know what a good teacher is, or how to hire one. And school principals don't know which of their teachers are good and which are bad.[9]

It's quite simple, really, to anyone with sense: The good teacher is the one who encourages, inspires, and ultimately causes children to learn. In the history of education there have been too few studies that compare student achievement with teacher attributes. The research that has been done is remarkable for what it does *not* show. It does not show that student achievement has been increased by any of the attributes valued by teacher colleges or school districts.

Should teachers be paid more because of the color of their hair, or the kind of bicycles they ride, or their height? Of course not, because these things have nothing to do with learning. Teacher salaries should be based on things that affect the quality of learning. Better teachers should be rewarded with more money; that's just common sense. But they are not.

In fact, every teacher salary schedule in the country is based on two things: years of experience and number of postcollege education classes taken. School districts have assumed that experience and education make for better teachers, so they have based pay scales on these two factors. Unfortunately, research has shown that their assumptions are false. They might as well base their salaries on shininess of teeth or on blood type, because these have as much effect on teaching ability as experience and education do.

Although it seems reasonable to assume that a teacher who has earned a master's degree or Ph.D. has learned enough to become a better teacher, the research does not confirm this assumption. There is no relation between the teacher's level of education and her students' level of achievement.[10]

In a famous case in Florida, teachers in one district

were replaced by housewives with no particular training. Without the supposed benefits of teaching experience or any kind of teaching courses, the housewives carried on the educational program smoothly, and the children achieved as much under their tutelage as they did with certified instructors. So much for the concept of teaching as an arcane profession that requires years of training and certification to keep out the riffraff. The truth is that most parents could step in and replace a teacher, and do a better job of it, too.

WHY SCHOOLS DON'T PUNISH INCOMPETENCE

A bad teacher is like a gorilla with body odor; the problem *could* be fixed, but not by you, and then only if the gorilla wants to improve. You can't fire the gorilla, because he's got a lawyer who is even bigger and smellier than he is. You can't get the zookeeper to do anything, because his job is to protect the gorilla; and anyway, the zookeeper lost his sense of smell years ago. He wouldn't know a sewer from a rose. The only real choice is for you to move upwind from the gorilla.

Why can't we fire the gorillas of the teaching profession? It is almost impossible to fire a public school teacher if she has taught more than three years. After about three years the teacher has tenure, which means that she has job security for life, regardless of the quality of her work.

A tenured teacher's job is protected by layers of laws and labor union support. To fire an incompetent teacher requires specific, hard evidence; it requires a lot of time to get through grievance processes and through the courts of law; and it requires lots of money. It would cost a school district at least $50,000, perhaps as much as

$300,000, to get rid of an incompetent teacher. Smaller school districts may find this too great a hardship. In school districts of *any* size, it is not surprising how rarely a teacher is fired.

In a year, the chances of a teacher being fired for incompetence are about 1 in 10,000. The most informed estimates are that 5 percent to 15 percent of teachers are incompetent. That means that for every 10,000 teachers, 500 to 1,500 are incompetent, but only one will be fired for incompetence, and the other 499 to 1,499 will continue to teach your children. So the American classroom becomes a permanent haven for the terminally incompetent. Even the gorilla needs a home.

But pity the poor children who have to share their classrooms daily with the gorillas. Children know nothing of tenure, or lawyers, or indifferent bureaucracies. All they want is a sympathetic adult who can channel their natural love of learning and sense of wonder. What they get is a jaded, aging timeserver with no hope of advancement and no fear of review, who is inspired only by the distant prospect of retirement. It's not a fair situation, and it is perpetuated only because the children lack a voice in their own behalf.

The entire educational hierarchy has no idea what makes for a good teacher. As a result, they don't reward the good ones, can't get rid of the bad ones, and can't even distinguish the good ones from the bad ones.

The Bad Teacher: Does Your Child Have One?

You know what a good teacher can be; a good teacher can be the catalyst who inspires enthusiasm for reading,

learning, and being an active participant in the classroom. She can be the foundation for a child's feelings of
competency and confidence. In a good teacher's classroom, the children tolerate each other's weaknesses and
are not crushed by their own.

But perhaps this year, your child is not in such an idyl-
lic classroom. You have sensed that something is wrong,
and you suspect that the teacher may be part of what is
wrong. Perhaps this chapter has described some classrooms like your own child's, and reading about them has
lit some Aha! lightbulbs above your head. The checklist
below summarizes some of the ways teachers can be bad.
Look for one or more of these indicators:

• The teacher comes preequipped with a bad reputation from other parents. The grapevine is a better rating
system than it gets credit for.

• The teacher doesn't seem very bright or very articulate. He avoids written communication or displays a poor
grasp of the subject matter.

• The teacher can't control classroom behavior. She
can't set up a system to allow for individualization or follow through on individual remediation plans.

• The teacher shows wide mood swings, anger, or vindictive behavior. Your child reports that the teacher
doesn't like him, or that he seems to "have it in" for a
particular child.

• The teacher can't diagnose specific learning problems. She seems unaware of symptoms of these problems,
and can't answer specific questions in parent-teacher
conferences.

• The teacher obsesses on method, focusing more on
the teaching process than on student learning. He ignores

or dismisses any parental input about the techniques that have worked for them.

• The teacher has inappropriate goals, or no goals, for the year. When asked about her goals, the teacher speaks of curricula or textbooks.

These are ways that a teacher can be bad for a whole classroom of children. But you must remember that your concern is only for your own child, and that must be so for two good reasons. First, you are the only person in the world who really cares about the education of your child. As we have seen, schools and teachers have other priorities, and your child's education may be low on their list of priorities. Second, you can save your child, or you can save all of the children, but you can't do both. That is, you can save your child by getting him away from a bad teacher; or you can save all the children by campaigning to get rid of the bad teacher. But the campaigning approach will take too long to benefit your own child.

So what do you do? Save your own.

Is that selfish? No, because if enough parents act to save their own, it has the same effectiveness as a campaign.

And how do you save your own? Partly by *not* using what you have learned about bad teachers. You can get what you want from the school system if you know more than you say. In the next chapters, you will learn what to say (and more important, what not to say) when pointing the finger at the bad teacher and talking with school officials. Most important, you will learn what you need to know to save your child from a complacent, ineffective teacher, without damaging your child's love of learning.

7

High Noon: Confronting the Teacher

High noon approaches. In the flickering blue light of the television screen, Gary Cooper prepares for the showdown. He knows the bad guys are out there and he knows he's outgunned. He faces certain defeat, but he cannot run from his duty. Despite the terrible odds, he knows that he must stand up, or else the forces of evil will trample the innocent and the defenseless. And he knows he will stand alone, because he alone has the backbone to face the bad guys.

As you sit before the television, you think about your own upcoming High Noon—the one at your son or daughter's school. Having submitted to a first "problem-solving" conference, and having survived at least one ineffective plan to improve your child's grades, behavior, or morale, you are now convinced that you know who the bad guy is; it's the teacher. He has created your child's problem, or contributed to it, or failed to do anything to help solve it.

He's a bad teacher, and he may have been a bad teacher for a long time, but he's still teaching. Perhaps

other parents never had the nerve to stand up and complain, or perhaps they complained and nobody listened.
Either way, the bad teacher continues to be bad. He is
damaging your child, and will damage other children in
the future. You feel like Gary Cooper in *High Noon,* knowing that someone has to stand up for the weak and defenseless, and anguished to realize that no one else seems
to have the backbone to do it.

And make no mistake about it: Confronting a teacher
requires a great deal of backbone. Marching alone into
battle against a teacher and his whole army of supporters
is a terrifying prospect. You have the feeling that whatever you say will be taken as an attack, and not just an
attack upon the teacher. In most schools, your feelings
would be correct. When you attack the teacher, the
school principal and then the superintendent may rush to
his defense. Before you know what hit you, it seems as
though the whole school district is telling you that your
accusations are unfounded, that you don't know anything
about the inner workings of education, and that only educational professionals have the training and knowledge
to criticize their peers. It's no wonder parents feel overwhelmed and outnumbered at the prospect of criticizing
a teacher. It's also understandable that parents who have
suffered through numerous conferences, ineffective "remediation plans," or any number of ill-conceived strategies that accomplished nothing for the child other than to
demoralize and isolate him, will simply choose to "get
through the rest of the year" any way they can; it's too
daunting to confront the teacher, even when they *know*
the teacher is the root of the problem.

If you are one of those parents, if soldiering through a
mountain of tear-stained homework papers and ticking

off the interminable school days between now and the third week of June seems somehow more tolerable to you than the thought of confronting a substandard teacher, I urge you to reconsider. There are three good reasons to act on your child's behalf.

First, a confrontation is neither an argument nor an ambush. It is merely an effort to bring the teacher face-to-face with the truth as you and your child see it. Confronting the teacher in this way—that is, calmly and diplomatically—need not be unpleasant for you or for the teacher.

Second, confronting the teacher will finally put an end to the bad teacher behaviors or useless strategies that are making school more difficult for your child. In earlier conferences, you agreed to the teacher's plan to improve your child; since then, you and your child have done your best to follow the plan. But grades and behavior have not improved, so clearly the teacher's plan is not working. There is no reason, other than teacher ineptitude or hostility, for the bad teacher to continue using methods that set your child apart, demean him, or compound his struggles.

The third, and in the long run perhaps the most important reason to take your complaint directly to the bad teacher, is that confronting him face-to-face is simply the right thing to do. Indeed, the ability to go straight to the source, state your grievance, and request correction is emblematic of mature, confident behavior. Talking about the teacher behind his back or muttering at PTA meetings is not. Moreover, addressing your concerns to the teacher is considered to be the correct protocol by most principals and superintendents; if you haven't gone directly to the teacher, they will ask why you have not. Should you need to enlist the help of the administrators, and you may, having attempted to handle your child's difficulty in a forthright and honest way will certainly enhance your credibility.

At this point, it can be tempting to burst in with both guns blazing, to attack the bad teacher verbally. After all, this man or woman may be responsible for wasting most of a year of your child's valuable educational life. The teacher may have made the "school-day stomachache" a chronic condition for your child. He or she may have diminished your child's love of learning, eroded her self-confidence, and affected your entire family's quality of life (just try to inspire some "family fun" when one little member of the family is moping over another dismal progress report or another teacher injustice). You have every right to be angry. But anger isn't likely to get you anywhere.

You can, however, make a successful show of strength, confront a bad teacher, and minimize the stress in your child's academic life. This chapter will show you how you can effectively argue your child's case with the teacher—without ever arguing at all. It will also teach you what results you can expect from the follow-up conference, how to move beyond the most common teacher defenses, and how to negotiate a more positive, mutual respectful teacher-student relationship for your child . . . to make life more livable for your child until you can get him out of the bad teacher's classroom and into a more secure learning environment. With this advice, you can achieve your goals and save your child without the trauma of a shoot-out at high noon.

Scheduling the Follow-up Conference

Marisa was not a particularly cuddly child, but there was no reason why the teacher should have singled her out for constant criticism, repeatedly reducing her to tears in the classroom. Marisa's mother was patient. She accepted the teacher's suggestion that Marisa was an "overly sensitive child who needed time to toughen up," at least for a while. But when time failed to stem the flood of tears, she asked for a follow-up conference with the teacher. The teacher scheduled the conference for 8:45 A.M. in her classroom.

When the mother arrived for the conference, she was aghast to see that Marisa and her classmates were already entering the classroom and taking their seats! The teacher, anticipating exactly what the conference was about, had set the stage in full view and earshot of the class. Under the circumstances, it was impossible for the mother to complain about Marisa's treatment without embarrassing her daughter. The teacher had used her "home field advantage."

In a very real sense, just calling the teacher to request a follow-up conference is a form of confrontation. The bad teacher is fully aware that he has been ineffective; he already knows that his "strategy," the one worked out at an earlier conference with you, has been a failure. In fact, the only surprise to the bad teacher is that you are initiating a second conference at all. He knows how eagerly most parents will avoid confrontation with a teacher. He knows that wise parents are reluctant to put pressure on an instructor, particularly an instructor who can return the pressure to the child, behind the closed doors of his classroom. As a result, your request to confer, and presumably to challenge the teacher, will come as some surprise. The teacher may interpret it as a threat, and it will almost certainly put the teacher on the defensive.

Nevertheless, as I have explained earlier, the parent-teacher conference is not a meeting of equals. And although the parent may have the element of surprise and a truckload of good intentions on her side, it is still Mom or Dad—and not the teacher—who is in the inferior position. The meeting will always be held on the teacher's home turf. Usually the meeting will be in the teacher's classroom where the teacher can control the interruptions, set the agenda, and dictate the scheduling. It is fruitless for a parent even to try to negotiate a meeting place away from the school, unless that parent is bedridden or otherwise immobilized.

As Marisa's story illustrates, however, the time of the meeting is crucial, and parents should not be passive in agreeing to whatever time the teacher suggests. Remember that the important time constraint is not the meeting's starting time; it's the *ending* time. The teacher wants a conference to last about twenty minutes. That's just long enough for an exchange of pleasantries and for the teacher to present his views and conclusions. It isn't long enough for the parents to initiate any meaningful dialogue or to respond effectively to the teacher's comments. So the teacher will schedule the conference so that after twenty minutes he can curtail it because of another obligation, such as a class or another conference. Then he can announce that the conference is ended, whether or not the parent has had her say or any agreement has been reached. Often, because of the time pressure, parents cannot verbalize the very complaints they came to voice.

They may even find themselves hastily agreeing to accept any resolution the teacher offers, before they have had time to think through the teacher's ideas or to make suggestions. When a teacher is anticipating a conference with a possibly hostile parent, he will schedule that conference before school or during his free periods, so he can control the time of adjournment.

If you are scheduling a follow-up conference, particularly one where you intend to delineate the failed performance of a teacher, you should insist on holding the meeting at the end of the school day. This gives you several advantages. First of all, it allows enough time for an open-ended discussion of the issues, including parents' opinions and not just the teacher's views. Second, it prevents the teacher from closing off discussion to fit her schedule. Finally, as the clock moves past the teacher's paid hours and into her personal time, the teacher may be the one who is willing to concede issues in order to conclude the conference. These factors work to the parents' advantage especially effectively on *Friday* afternoons.

If the teacher does not want to meet after school, offer to meet him away from school. When he objects, point out that you are trying to be reasonable, and that he should try to meet you halfway. Then perhaps you can compromise on a meeting at school at the end of the day, which is what you wanted in the first place. If he insists on a meeting before or during school, don't agree unless he is willing to schedule a whole series of conference times, enough meetings to cover the topics to *your* satisfaction. In other words, don't let his schedule dictate the terms of any agreement *you* might want to make.

If she insists that the meeting be held at her time and location, you should insist that the meeting not be held in the classroom and that the school principal provide classroom coverage if the meeting should last longer than the teacher wants it to last. Again, this is to prevent her from announcing that the conference is over before you are ready to end it, or otherwise manipulating you with her scheduling constraints.

Preparing for the Conference

This conference will not be the congenial get-acquainted conference discussed earlier. Nor will it be the cooperative think tank you held when you first discussed your child's problems. Although you have exerted every effort to make them succeed, the teacher's ideas on how to help your child have not worked. They may even have made the situation worse. In any event, you are certain now that it is the teacher, not the pupil, who is the failure.

You were advised, before your first conference, to have some goals in mind ahead of time; and that's still true. But this time, your goals will be different. If, for example, your desire for the meeting derives from outrage at the awful way your child is being treated, consider this: If your goal for the meeting is to repay the abuse that has been heaped on your child, what happens next? After you have raked the teacher over the coals, what will happen the next day, or the next week? Have you made your child's life easier?

John L. was a good boy, but he was not so good a student. Socially, he was at the bottom of the pecking order.

The other children picked on him and the teacher wouldn't do anything about it. John's mother went to school and angrily attacked the teacher for her inaction. After that, the teacher pointedly ignored the problem, thereby encouraging the children to continue picking on John L. It took three years of therapy for John L. to recover from those ten months of abuse.

In brief, venting your frustration and anger may be therapeutic for you but can only complicate the problem for your child. Therefore, although you are here to make your opinions known, the opportunity to vent your emotions should not be your goal for the conference. Set goals that are practical for both your child and the teacher, and focus on the kinds of alternatives that the teacher is capable of providing (if he is *willing* to do so).

What commitments can you ask for, and what can you reasonably expect to get from this follow-up teacher conference? Keep in mind that the best long-term option may be to have your child removed from the inept teacher's classroom. Here are some short-term suggestions that may improve your child's classroom experience immediately, until a long-term solution can be arranged:

• You can ask for a change in the teacher's attitude and behavior, if they are what you believe is creating a problem for your child.

• You can ask for a change in the teacher's response to your child's behavior, if his current responses have proven unhelpful.

• You can ask for a change in the teacher's attitude toward your child's academic performance, if her current attitude is destructive to your child.

• You can ask for a change in your child's seating or

grouping within the class, if your child's peer relationships are part of the problem.

• You can ask for more time and attention for your child, in the form of in-class or after-class help or pull-out programs. The time and attention might come from peer tutoring, reading or math specialists, teacher's aides, teacher interns, or the teacher himself.

• You can ask for special assignments for your child, whether it is extra work for enrichment or skill-building work for remediation.

• You can ask for special record keeping or assignment checking if your child's problem is behavior or a study skills deficiency.

• You can ask for further testing, especially if you and the teacher disagree on the definition of your child's problem.

• You can ask that your child be transferred to another classroom. The teacher does not have the power to authorize this transfer, but she can start the process moving.

You aren't going to get everything you ask for, and you may not get anything. But it's guaranteed that if you don't ask, you won't get. And it's important to put it on the record that you *did ask*.

Your goal in the follow-up conference is to get the teacher to see your point of view of your child's problem, and to take whatever action is necessary to solve the problem. A reasonable teacher will try hard to understand your viewpoint and to help with whatever resources he has available. The bad teacher may deny the validity of your viewpoint and withhold all the resources he can.

The Teacher's Point of View

The teacher will certainly come into the conference with some goals of her own, and they will assuredly have nothing in common with yours. At this point, your child has been damaged by that teacher, so you will have very little sympathy for the teacher's goals, whatever they might be. You don't care if she never reaches her goals, and you have no desire to help her achieve anything. But you must act in the best interests of your child; and to give you the best possible bargaining position, you should try to understand the teacher's point of view, and then formulate a plan that helps your child but also enables the teacher to reach her goals. For example, if you suggest a plan for your child that means more work for the teacher, the teacher will resist. But if the same plan is cast as a way to enhance the teacher's reputation as a problem solver, she is more likely to agree to it.

What does the teacher want?

First, the teacher wants a sense that her life has value, that she is doing something worthwhile. Many teachers have the poster or the coffee cup that reads, "A Teacher Affects Eternity." The idea that she could make the world a better place is what attracted her to teaching in the first place. She feels that she has turned her back on income and social standing in order to help the world as a teacher, and she wants parents to appreciate her self-sacrifice. Even the bad teachers, those who have not devoted effort or dedication to their teaching, expect parents to be grateful for the *time* they have sacrificed.

Second, the teacher wants the sense that he does his job well. He wants to be respected by his peers and his bosses for the quality of his work. He would like to have parents say, to him or to others, that he is really helping their child. In teaching, excellence is rewarded by neither promotion nor higher salaries, so excellent teachers like to be rewarded by praise. Bad teachers are equally gratified by praise, and probably won't notice that the praise is insincere. Teachers, particularly the bad ones, feel threatened by articulately irate parents because those parents can impair their self-esteem as well as their professional reputations with their colleagues.

Third, the teacher wants a sense of control over her world. She has created a microcosm in her classroom in which she is the supreme being. Teachers like the feeling of control, and are often resentful of interference from administrators and bureaucratic regulations. You will recognize this kind of teacher by her cry: "If they would only leave me alone and let me teach."

The teacher, having established her control over her little world, wants that control to continue. She may feel threatened by lively students who disrupt her class (which may be why you are having this conference). She may even attempt to close off any avenues of parental interference or involvement.

The parent should be aware, in negotiating, that the teacher's goal may be to have no changes in her well-ordered little world. She doesn't want any additional burden of time or effort that may strain her control over the classroom. She certainly doesn't want the parent to do anything that would cause her boss to increase his supervision of her, because that would destroy her feeling of control.

Parents should also be aware that there is a dark side to the teacher's need for control. Some saintly clergymen are called to serve God; some pompous ones feel called to play God. Some people aspire to be policemen because they want the license to be bullies with badges. Some people aspire to be teachers, not from altruism or a love of children, but because it gives them the opportunity to play God with people smaller and less powerful than themselves. All of us, especially children, need to be protected from people with a pathological need for control.

Parents should also be aware of some other factors that influence teachers. It is important to note that bad teachers are often the ones less capable of dealing with these influences, including:

Loneliness: The classroom teacher interacts with few other adults in the course of his day. He may not have anyone with whom to discuss his problems, frustrations, and triumphs. Some teachers are more at ease socially with children than with other adults. They may express their feelings inappropriately to their students.

Hopelessness: Many teachers must deal with too many kids and too many social problems, and they are expected to achieve too many goals set by too many social reformers. The task is so overwhelming and the chance of success so minimal, that it is easy for a sense of hopelessness to prevail. And in the rare cases when the teacher succeeds, her students move on to the next grade, and a new crop of impossible problems takes their place. For the hopeless teacher, moving forward is like walking into the ocean, each step taking her in farther over her head.

Hostility: Every teacher faces frustrations in all parts of his life: dealing with the children, dealing with his bosses, dealing with his personal life. Sometimes, in the bad teacher, these frustrations contribute to a general feeling of hostility, which might be expressed through sarcasm, defensiveness, suspicion, temperament, hypersensitivity, or prejudice. A teacher who has collected a heavy load of hostility may lash out at a child or class for no reason or for insufficient reason.

Idealism: Many teachers have an idealized concept of what a teacher should be. Of course, being human, they never quite reach the ideal. For some teachers, there is great anguish in contemplating the gap between their fallible selves and the ideal teacher, a gap that they can never bridge.

All these influences that create problems in the bad teacher are factors over which you, as a parent, have no control. You can't make the teacher more stable or more able to cope with his or her world. And these feelings of loneliness, hopelessness, hostility, and unattainable idealism make the teacher feel guilty about the things they have done, or have not done, or ought to have done. A bad teacher's guilt causes her to be defensive, even when no one is attacking. And when a real attack like yours comes along, it brings out a teacher's defensive reactions in full flower.

Last-Ditch Teacher Defenses

The bad teacher knows he is bad. The plan he devised to transform your child into a higher-achieving or more compliant student has not worked. He knows that concocting a new and truly effective plan would require more time and more effort than he wants to or is able to give. It may require more brains than he has, or more self-control than he is willing to exert. And now, since you have asked for a follow-up conference, he knows that you know all of this, too. Devoid of any real ideas, without the slightest hint of how to aid a struggling child, the teacher becomes desperate to maintain the status quo, change as little as possible, and do as little as possible. Bad teachers have developed a variety of strategies to keep parents from disrupting their lives or forcing them to confront their own failures. Parents, especially those who are confronting a teacher or questioning his motives and methods, need to be aware of these strategies and look for them during the conferences. Forewarned and forearmed, parents should be able to get past the teacher's defenses so they can bring effective help to their child. Some standard teacher defenses are:

The Blame the Victim Defense You have established, to your own satisfaction, that your child's problem is the teacher. The teacher, of course, would not agree with this; it would never even occur to her. The teacher defends herself by condemning the child. She points to poor performance in the grade book, as if the result were the cause. She reports on his bad behavior, ignoring her role in provoking the bad behavior. She suggests solutions to the problem, always things that the *child* must change or the *child* must do, based on the (sometimes unspoken) assumption that the *child* is the problem. You need to be very careful in battling this defense and its myriad variations. Of course, you want to tell her that changing the child's actions won't matter because *she* is the one at fault. But accusing such a teacher directly would be like waving a red flag in a bull's face. Instead, you must restrict yourself to suggesting things the teacher could do differently, and you must do it without appearing confrontational.

The Mr. Chips Defense The teacher will tell you that he is aware of the problem, is sympathetic to the problem, and is doing everything he can to help. He will give you a litany of all the things he is doing to help, inferring that he is already doing all that can be done, and that the next step is up to the child (or you). He hopes you won't notice that all those things he is doing are not relevant to the real problem and have not been successful anyway. Thank him for his efforts and then ask whether any of his efforts have shown results or have affected the real problem.

The Stonewall Defense Don't expect an in-depth discussion of your child's problem from the stonewalling teacher. She won't acknowledge that a problem exists. Even if she does acknowledge the problem, she certainly won't accept any responsibility for having caused it or contributed to it. She won't willingly schedule a conference, hiding behind labor contract clauses and school policies, and citing schedule conflicts to avoid meeting with parents. When forced to meet, the stonewaller will offer no suggestions, no help in solving the problem, and no hope of remediation for Billy. She will deny that anything she did could have caused or worsened the problem, and challenge you to prove otherwise. To deal with this defense, you need to be prepared with good documentation (see the next chapter), and be prepared to include the principal in the conference.

The Dr. Jekyll Defense This teacher is cooperative and easy for parents to deal with. He will agree with the parents in diagnosing the problem and in planning solutions. Then, as soon as Dr. Jekyll leaves the conference, he resumes his alter ego and forgets all the comments and promises he made. In extreme cases, he may present the Mr. Hyde face to the children, bullying them and being vindictive.

Before you finish any parent-teacher conference with the charming and agreeable Dr. Jekyll, it is important to schedule the follow-up meeting so you can be sure that the changes you agreed to are actually being implemented. This becomes really critical when you are dealing with a Jekyll-Hyde. The immediate prospect of the next meeting puts a short leash on his vindictiveness.

The Old Lady Who Lives In a Shoe Defense This teacher may acknowledge that there is a problem, but her response will be to throw up her hands and say, "What can I do? There are just too many children and not enough time to give them each attention. I would like to help your Tommy, but I don't have enough hands." In other words, your Tommy will learn nothing, but that's okay because all the other children will learn nothing, too.

A variation of this is the White Rabbit Defense: no time, no time, no time for preparation of special assignments for Amanda, no time for classroom attention to Amanda's needs. These teachers need to brush up on their classroom management skills. They might also think about the sign commonly found in many offices: "Failure to plan ahead on your part does not constitute an emergency on my part."

The Large-Mouth Bass Defense In this defense, the teacher is fishing around for a definition of the problem or for a solution. His plan is to stall, watch, and wait; try some minor change and watch it for a month to see if it has any effect. If not, try another minor variation and watch and wait. It won't solve the problem, but it will get him closer to June, when he can pass your Jessica on to the next teacher. The solution to this defense is a good offense; if he is vague about the problem or the solution, jump right in with your definition of the problem and your specific suggestions for solving the problem. He may live by the axiom "Don't just do something! Stand there!" But if you have solutions, he will need very good reasons to ignore them, and that will at least start a dialogue.

The William Buckley Defense This defense, the propagation of obfuscation, has been advocated by the Antioch School District in California: "Using a variety of words to describe a program or strategy and rotating to a new synonym they haven't picked up on seems to slow them [the parents] down." Teachers under siege may take refuge in educational jargon when questioned on any subject, but you can stop them by playing the bumpkin. Apologize for your "ignorance" and humbly ask them to explain their ideas in simple little words; that will blow away their smoke screen and make them say what they mean in plain English.

The purpose of most of these defenses is to shift responsibility: to shift responsibility for *causing* the problem from the teacher to the student; and to shift the responsibility for *solving* the problem from the teacher to the parent. The teacher will offer solutions that consist entirely of things the child and parent should do, like more tutoring, more time spent on homework, more counseling ... any solution that doesn't involve more work for the teacher.

In the end, you will be the one responsible for solving your child's problem, because you are the only one who truly cares whether it is solved. If you depend on the teacher to do it, it won't get done. Nevertheless, it is crucial that you negotiate some effort by the school, too. If the problem is in your child but was caused or worsened by the school, then you will need to see some changes made at the school. They have a legal responsibility to educate children; if they refuse to shoulder that responsibility, then they should close their doors and end the hypocrisy.

The Showdown

All the preliminaries are done. You have scheduled the meeting, made a list of your goals for the meeting, considered the teacher's perspective and her goals, and thought about defeating the teacher's defenses. You are almost prepared for the meeting itself. There is only one more issue to consider before confronting the teacher: your own emotions.

You don't want a showdown at high noon in the middle of the street. You would rather have a friendly conversation that leaves everyone feeling good. So you should go in with a positive attitude and, if you can still muster one, a smile.

You should start the conference with small talk. Compliment the appearance of her room, admire the picture of her family, find something to approve of. Beginning with

positive personal comments makes it easier to have a reasoned discussion later. Ask her questions, even personal
questions; people love to talk about themselves and their
work. And as she answers your questions you should listen, not for the facts in her answers, but for the values,
attitudes, and intentions in her answers. As you listen,
don't be judgmental; if you appear open-minded, she will
be encouraged to open up. The more she talks, the more
she will reveal, so let her talk. Let *her* fill the awkward
silences.

Never use your questions to show off how smart you
are, or to show how much you know about her. In fact,
don't do anything to show how smart you are. It is always better to play dumb and let the teacher underesti-
mate you.

When the teacher asks you questions, remember that
you are not her student. You do not have to please the
teacher or even answer her questions. Give her only
whatever information you choose to share. Remember,
too, the teacher now knows that the jig is up. You have
found her to be incompetent. In order to save face, she
may begin fishing for information she can use to discredit
you or your child. Stay calm and pleasant, but quiet. You
need not help the teacher build a case against your child
or against yourself.

In this pressured situation, it is possible that the
teacher will make a comment about herself or your child
that is so outrageously false that you want to respond
with anger. It isn't easy to hear a teacher put the blame
on a second-grader—especially when it's a second-grader
you happen to love. But an angry explosion will not make
life better for your little one, and could easily make her
life worse.

For the sake of your child, you must control your anger. Here are some suggestions of things you can do to keep the conference going in a constructive and positive way, when you would really rather sink your teeth into the teacher.

First, refer to your notes. A written list of what you hoped to achieve from this meeting will keep you focused on the problem rather than on your emotions. Remember, it's about Johnny. Before you speak in anger, ask yourself, "Will this help Johnny get the help he needs?" Keep the focus on the future, not on the past.

Second, avoid statements that begin with "You . . ." Sentences that take on an accusatory tone, however valid, will cause the teacher to dig in his heels and fight you. Instead, use "I . . ." statements that reveal your feelings ("I am frustrated by Johnny's lack of progress in science") or statements that give your child's perception of the problem ("Jill feels that you don't like her"). The message will be the same, but the teacher will find the language less threatening.

Sometimes when the teacher wants to blame the child, it is helpful for the parent to take the heat in place of the child: "Oh, I'm sorry. Timmy did that because I told him to . . ." As parents, we can carry the blame better than the little ones can; and it gives the teacher less chance to make the child look guilty. It also sends the message that "Timmy may be too naive to see your blame-shifting game, but you haven't fooled us parents."

A third way to control your anger and avoid messy confrontations is to speak abstractly. Don't speak directly of this teacher and her specific failures. Instead, speak of the teacher in the third person. Use hypothetical situations, asking how a child should respond if a teacher does this or that. You could be even more abstract, referring to the *school* rather than to the *teacher*; how should a child respond when this or that happens at *school?* You could ask how the ideal teacher would react to a child's actions or performance; this has the benefit of subtly reminding the teacher how far she is from the ideal.

Here are some examples of parent-teacher follow-up conferences on the brink of explosion, and how you can keep the peace.

THE SITUATION: In an earlier conference you explained to the teacher that your daughter is sensitive and is upset by loud voices, but the teacher continues to yell at the kids.

WHAT YOU WANT TO SAY: "Pick on somebody your own size, you big bully! How would you like it if your boss yelled at you in front of all the other teachers?"

WHAT YOU SHOULD SAY: "Children get upset when they are yelled at for something that isn't their fault. It offends their sense of fair play. What should children do when a teacher yells at them?"

THE SITUATION: If Suzie doesn't understand something, she raises her hand and asks. Lately when Suzie has a question, the teacher rolls her eyes and says that Suzie wasn't paying attention—again.

WHAT YOU WANT TO SAY: "Suzie didn't understand that problem? You don't seem to understand *this* problem that you are causing for Suzie. Should I make you appear stupid or inattentive? Should I yell at you because you don't under-stand?"

WHAT YOU SHOULD SAY: "We've always taught Suzie that the only stupid question is the one she doesn't ask. So often, there are other children who also don't understand. Isn't it brave of Suzie to raise her hand? She's the one who is willing to admit that she and the others need a little extra help. Don't you think a girl like that should be encour-aged?"

THE SITUATION: Independent testing has found evidence of a specific learning disability, and you are hopeful that your child will now begin to fulfill his potential. But the teacher, who never diagnosed the problem in the first place, is not doing anything to accommodate your child's specific needs.

WHAT YOU WANT TO SAY: "You were too blind to recognize his problem, and now you are too stupid and too lazy to do anything about it!"

WHAT YOU SHOULD SAY: "It is such a joy to see a child blossoming like a flower. It makes me proud to be part of the growing process. The experts have suggested a few changes that could really change Bobbie's life. . . . Is there any problem with making those changes in your classroom?"

THE SITUATION: The teacher says that your child is the only one in the class who is having his particular problem.

WHAT YOU WANT TO SAY: "You are either a liar or an idiot. I'm not even in your classroom and I know of several children with the same problem as Ben."

WHAT YOU SHOULD SAY: "Isn't that interesting. He has never struggled with that subject before. Why do you suppose there is a problem now?"

THE SITUATION: The class is behind in math (or reading, etc.).

WHAT YOU WANT TO SAY: "Whatever you are doing isn't working. Are you too stupid or too obstinate to try something else? Is the class behind in math because you don't understand math, or because you don't know how to teach it?"

WHAT YOU SHOULD SAY: "I am concerned because Jenny's math skills are still low, even after the remedial drills you suggested. Is the class spending enough time on math? What do you think of the textbooks? Is there more material that might be helpful in the teacher's editions? What is Miss Paragon [better teacher, same grade] doing differently? What can we do that we have not done before?"

THE SITUATION: The teacher's suggested solution for your child's problem is to do more of the same—more studying, more time on homework, more tutoring . . .

WHAT YOU WANT TO SAY: "You wouldn't know it's raining unless your car floated away! Look around you! What you are doing is not working! You don't even understand what the problem is!"

WHAT YOU SHOULD SAY: "If that doesn't work, what else could be tried? We have already established that your first suggestion hasn't worked, so let's go straight to your second suggestion."

∞

THE SITUATION: The teacher has been around for a long time, and no longer has any sensitivity to children's needs and fears.

WHAT YOU WANT TO SAY: "You're a decrepit old jackass and you've run your classroom like a tyrant for thirty years. Why don't you retire and stop destroying my child's self-esteem?"

WHAT YOU SHOULD SAY: "Diana says she's too stupid to succeed in your class. She feels inadequate and nervous, and she's lost her eagerness to learn. What do you suppose could have made her feel that way? What can the school do to help?"

Including the Child

Should the child be present at the follow-up conference? There are good reasons for and against including your child in the conference, and you will just have to play it by ear. Your child's learning process will be smoother if he has the impression that parents and teacher are on the same team, so any part of the conference that involves conflict should certainly not include the child. And any agreement that parents and teachers make may involve compromise; it's better that the child remain unaware of the bargaining positions that led to the compromise.

On the other hand, it may be wise to include the child in at least part of the conference. The child is your "expert witness," the only one on your side who can give an eyewitness account. Including him allows you to observe the student-teacher interaction: Is your child intimidated by the teacher or can he speak up and tell his tale? Does the teacher listen patiently to her student, or does she interrupt and overrule him? Whatever chemistry exists between teacher and pupil should quickly become apparent to you.

Having student and teacher meet face-to-face also keeps each from telling tales behind the other's back. It ensures that events are recounted without editing or embellishment, and makes the truth more compelling.

The best advice is to include the child in part of the meeting, but certainly not in any part that is confrontational. You should start the meeting without him and set a tone of professionalism, honesty, and cooperation. Try to establish some tentative areas of agreement. Then you should tell the teacher that you want your child to join your meeting and establish some ground rules about what will be discussed (and what will not be discussed) in his presence. Do not spring any surprises on the teacher while the child is there; if you do, you destroy any possibility of working with that teacher. (Even if you have decided to remove your child from that classroom or school, you need the teacher's help to make the child's transition as smooth as possible.) And never use the child to "testify" in support of your angry accusations of the teacher. You will provoke the teacher to vindictiveness and ensure that your child will learn less during the time he remains in her classroom.

Whatever agreement you may reach with the teacher is not just an agreement between parent and teacher; it's an agreement among parent, teacher, and child. After all, if the parents and teacher do their parts to meet the terms of the agreement but the child doesn't do her part, the agreement will fail. The child has to "sign on" to meeting her responsibilities, so the child has to be present for that part of the conference.

In the child's absence, you and the teacher need to discuss and agree on the next step—what to do if these plans don't solve the problem. The child should not be included in this part of the discussion. If he were, he could deliberately sabotage this plan because he prefers another alternative.

Concluding the Conference

The parent-teacher conference is winding down to a successful conclusion. You followed the advice in this chapter by scheduling the conference at a time that allowed full discussion by both sides; you kept your eye on the prize, always focusing on specific goals; you kept calm and learned by listening; and you extracted as much as possible from the other side. Is it time to shake hands and go home? Not yet.

After you have come to an agreement and while you are still in the meeting, you should state the areas of agreement verbally, so there is no confusion about what has been agreed to. You may wish to make written notes that specify *who* has agreed to do *what, under what conditions,* and *when.* Because you are dealing with a bad teacher, it is especially important to write down exactly what the teacher has agreed to do—or to *stop* doing.

Before you adjourn the meeting you should set a date for a follow-up. If this meeting did not produce agreement, you should schedule another meeting as soon as possible. If the meeting did produce agreement (and you should remain doubtful of the efficacy of any agreement reached at this point), schedule a meeting two or three weeks in the future, with the option to reduce it to a phone meeting if the plan seems to be succeeding. If the plan calls for further information and/or observation, specific dates should be established for that; usually about one week. Parents should beware of delaying tactics that schools like to use, so they should never leave the conference without fixed dates for the follow-up meetings.

After the meeting, the parent should write and send a "memo of agreement" to the teacher. It should identify the original areas of parent concern, summarize the areas of discussion, and specify points of agreement. It should spell out who has agreed to do what and when. Since the parent is the one writing the memo, the parent can include the specific bad behaviors the teacher has agreed to relinquish. If discussed and agreed upon, the memo should specify the next steps that would be triggered when these plans prove ineffective.

A copy of the memo of agreement should be sent to the school principal or the school office, with a request that it become part of the student's file. The teacher may respond to your memo and is entitled to place her response in that same file; in that case, you are entitled to a copy of her response. It is important to put all of this on the record because it documents your case when, as is likely, you need to carry your complaint to a higher court.

The follow-up conference has been quite different from your earlier parent-teacher conferences. The agreements that resulted from the earlier conferences were largely lists of things that you and your child needed to do, with minimal requirements for the teacher. The follow-up conference, if it reaches any agreement at all, is more likely to list things the *teacher* is required to do (or change). And that is the weak link in the agreement.

You have control over yourself and, to a significant extent, control over your child; but you have no control over the teacher. And by this time, you know that the teacher is unqualified, so you need to remain skeptical of the new agreement's chances of success. You have bought your child some time, and perhaps made the classroom temporarily more tolerable, but it's unlikely that you have found a long-term solution to your child's problem. Keep your eyes and ears open, and look ahead to your next step, which will probably involve working with the school principal.

8

The Principal

" 'If you have a problem or a question, don't think twice—just pick up the phone and call me.' That's what the principal of my daughter's school always said on Back-to-School Night and at the class plays. . . . So when I'd finally taken all I could from my daughter's arrogant, hostile teacher, I did just what he had said to do—I picked up the phone and dialed his number. But the instant the phone started to ring, I began wondering. . . . Did he really care about the problems of one first-grader? Did he really mean for me to call? Or was that just something he said to make himself appear interested and accessible?"

The frustrated mother who recounted this experience had a point. Some school administrators are truly hands-on men and women. They sincerely welcome contact with their students and the parents of those students—even when the reason for that contact isn't entirely positive. Other principals are more like those old "friends" you occasionally bump into on the street—the ones who smile and insist, "Let's get together one day soon," then show no interest in following up with an actual meeting.

Whether the principal is sincere or not, sometimes parents have concerns that make it necessary for a parent to speak with her and expect results. Any problems that are not restricted to a single classroom (for example, the curriculum or test scores for an entire grade or the whole school) would fall into the principal's domain. Likewise, if the parent has a safety concern that affects the entire student body, or if the parent wants to volunteer a gift or service to the entire school, then she would speak to the principal rather than the classroom teacher.

Sometimes a good teacher will refer you to the principal, because she knows your child needs something that is beyond the scope of her authority to provide. She may suspect a learning disability, for example, but can't authorize the extensive testing or psychological counseling necessary to diagnose it properly (in most schools teachers can recommend this but not authorize it unilaterally). Another good teacher might want to arrange for some special service for your child that requires a waiver of school district policy. A teacher can't change district rules without permission from her boss.

Or there may be conflicts between teachers that create problems for your child; only the principal can resolve the problems because only the principal has authority over those teachers. For example, there may be schedule conflicts that prevent your child from getting the help he needs. Or teachers may disagree over who should give your child the help he is entitled to. Or teachers may give conflicting orders or set conflicting standards, making it impossible for your child to please everyone, and creating enormous stress on him.

Most important, if your child has a bad teacher, a teacher who seems to be an obstruction to your child's learning, then you just have to go over the teacher's head. And that means dealing with the principal. You will need the principal to act as boss, to make the teacher do the things she should be doing anyway. Eventually, you will need the principal, because only the principal can transfer your child to another class. Similarly, if your child has a good teacher who happens to be a bad match for your child, only the principal can make the necessary transfers.

You need the principal, but he doesn't necessarily need you. You are about to interrupt his normal routine and ask him to make some change that could upset his school or his teachers. This will not be the first time he has had to protect his school from "disruptive" influences like you, and he has lots of experience in defending the status quo. You are more likely to get a fair hearing from him if you have already established a positive relationship with him, so he will be less likely to think of you as a nuisance or even as an enemy.

The Principal: To Know Him Is to Have a Fighting Chance

Pity the poor child who has to suffer the effects of bad teaching. The holes in his bag of knowledge can be patched in a month, or a year, or a decade, but the scars left on his soul may last forever. It is much easier to smash an eggshell than to repair one; one teacher's heavy hand may require years of delicate rebuilding. For this reason, it is important that you cultivate a relationship with the school principal, because once a year he does something that is critically important to your child—he assigns him to a classroom and teacher for the next year.

In most schools, even those that pay lip service to "parent involvement," parents have no voice whatsoever in any decision that is really important to a child's educational well-being. Since choosing your child's teacher is probably the single most critical decision that affects your child's education, of course the school will not let you have any voice in the matter. Why do schools prevent parents from choosing teachers for their children? Simply because all of the parents would choose the good teachers and none would choose the bad ones. Then the principal would be forced to make an unpleasant decision. She would either have to recognize that she has an inferior teacher and try to get rid of him, or make twenty-five families unhappy by assigning their children to the inferior teacher. Rather than face such a choice, she avoids it. She remembers that when Henry Ford was the only supplier of low-priced automobiles, he could tell the customer, "You can have any color Model T, as long as it is black." Like Ford, the principal knows she is the town's only supplier of her particular product, low-priced education, so she doesn't have to satisfy the customer either. Her attitude may be polite, but the essence of her message is, "Shut up and take what we give you, and be thankful we're giving you anything at all."

It is a message that does not leave much room for dissent, argument, or even conversation. However, there are ways to have a voice in the process. The simplest and most obvious way is to go directly to the principal and simply ask that your child be assigned to the teacher you prefer.

The principal will undoubtedly respond with a standard speech about how children are assigned arbitrarily, or according to some time-honored or shopworn policy over which he has no control. School administrators try to pretend that teacher assignment is a bloodless clerical decision, and to them it *is* bloodless. They aren't the ones whose lives will be changed by the decision, whose home life, self-esteem, and belief in the future will be shaped by their decision. To those really affected by the choice of teacher, it is an injury and an insult to be left out of the choice-making process.

Nevertheless, you should sit there politely and pretend that you believe him when he says it is out of his hands. Thank him for listening to you, and let him know that you sincerely hope the luck of the draw will assign your child to the best teacher.

Regardless of what the principal says about how class assignments are made, in reality teachers and the principal sit down and make personal judgments about which child should go in which class. Even if the school really does assign classes by some automatic process, they also have a personal review of the results of that process, to ensure that each class reflects the right mix of boys and girls, scholars and troublemakers. And they do make changes (even if they deny it). Having made your feelings known, you hope that one of the changes might be in your favor.

Of course, your chances of getting the teacher you want are much better if you can give specific reasons why your child needs to be assigned to that teacher.

Don't say, "I want Mr. Topps because he is the best." You are implying that you are entitled to the best. The principal would never say it out loud, but her unspoken reaction would be, "Everyone is entitled to the best, and Mr. Topps definitely is the best. But I can't assign everyone to Mr. Topps. Why should I assign your child rather than someone else?"

Your reasons must have nothing to do with the superiority of Mr. Topps or the inferiority of the other teachers. If the principal were to give in to that line of reasoning, she would be admitting publicly that she has some inferior teachers. She would never admit that, because that would create other problems for her. Instead, offer the principal sound educational reasons why your child would fit better in your preferred teacher's class. Say, for example:

"Johnny needs the kind of [structured, open, warm, well-planned] classroom that Mr. Topps runs so well."

"Johnny is weaker in [math, reading, writing], which is just where Mr. Topps is at his best as a teacher. Johnny had a bad year with last year's teacher, and he needs to catch up in that subject."

Or, "Johnny is going through an emotional time now because of [divorce, single parent, new sibling, etc.] and needs a particularly supportive classroom environment. Since Mr. Topps has a background in counseling, I feel he's just the kind of teacher who can help my child blossom."

Posing your argument this way makes it clear to the principal that Mr. Topps would be very good for your child. It also helps to make the point that your child would be good for Mr. Topps—that his needs would call forth the teacher's strengths, which in turn would enhance the learning experience of the entire class. Placing Johnny in Mr. Topps's class would bring out the best in everyone.

It bears repeating here that your chances of winning the principal over are better if he knows you . . . and the parents whom the principal knows best are those who have "bought" the school. Although the idea sounds overtly calculating, the simple truth is that if you are the parent who supplied the terrarium for your child's classroom or donated a personal computer to the library, there will be a desire on the part of the school to keep you happy. But buying the school doesn't necessarily require you to reach for your wallet. If you have served the school in other, nonfinancial ways like volunteering in the school library or reading to the kindergarteners, there will be the same desire to keep you happy and repay you for the kindness you have shown the school. The ethics of this system are debatable; in being kind to you, is the school being fair to others? You don't know, and you didn't make the gifts expecting a quid pro quo, but it's human nature to favor friends over strangers. And it's hard to object to a little favoritism if it gets you a teacher who won't destroy your child.

There is one caveat, however. If you are active in the PTA or Parents' Association, the principal may be less likely to offend you but may also be careful not to favor you in any way that is too publicly obvious. You may request the best teacher for your child, but you are unlikely to get her if the powers that be have to bend some established policy for you. Every school will make exceptions "in the best interest of the child" but can't appear to make exceptions only for the most politically powerful or socially favored parents. The school wants to maintain its pose as the impartial authority on matters educational, so it will respond in good faith to requests but not to public or political pressure.

If you are a PTA leader, your child's teacher will be aware that you are often in contact with the principal, and that your PTA may be doing things cooperatively with the school or at the principal's request. Common sense tells the teacher to be particularly attentive to Johnny, if Johnny's parent has the principal's ear.

Needs: Your Child's, Yours, and the Principal's

Things are getting worse in Mrs. Jackson's class. Betty isn't learning much and she comes home unhappy most days. Betty has a rotten teacher who has been stonewalling you. Mrs. Jackson absolutely will not admit any responsibility for causing Betty's problem, and she refuses to do anything to help her. She will not offer the time and extra effort that Betty needs, and she will not change the behavior that is so destructive to Betty's education.

You know you have to go to the principal, because things simply cannot go on this way. The parent cannot force the teacher to do her job properly, but the *principal* can if he chooses to. If the principal won't make the teacher do her job properly, then it is time to get Betty away from that teacher! Again, only the principal has the power to separate Betty from that teacher by transferring one or the other to a different classroom.

When you go to the school principal, you will be asking him to do something he really doesn't want to do—make a change. His needs don't coincide with yours. He wants to keep his staff happy, retain his control over a stable workplace, and look good to his supervisor. If you want to succeed, you must find a way for him to serve his own needs by serving yours.

The principal is not going to do anything for you just because you ask him to. His path of least resistance is to do nothing, and that's just what he will do unless you give him a good reason to do otherwise. If you antagonize him, he will dig in his heels and resist your efforts. You must appear as cooperative as possible because he is bigger and stronger than you are, and has access to more weapons than you have. Your best plan is to make him feel that helping you is what he wants to do.

There is an old adage: "Trying to teach a pig to fly is a waste of time, and besides, it annoys the pig." Well, asking the principal to do things that principals just don't do is a waste of time—and besides, it annoys the principal.

The typical elementary school principal is a former teacher, but not one of the really bad ones who inspired this book. He was a good manager who ran a quiet classroom and did not generate audible complaints from parents. His classroom was visually pleasing and had attractive bulletin boards. He got along well with other teachers and with officials at school district headquarters. He displayed leadership for other teachers in meetings for textbook selection and other projects, not including any projects where student growth could be measured.

This principal achieved his present position by avoiding conflict and by resolving conflicts around him. He knows that some (maybe many) of the teachers are incompetent, but he also knows that dealing with the problem would be unpleasant, unrewarding, and probably unsuccessful. The principal wants to stay as happy as a pig in mud, and he does it by not trying to teach his own pigs to fly. The principal leaves the incompetent teachers alone and pats himself on the back for being virtuously nonjudgmental.

As a part of avoiding confrontation with incompetent teachers, the principal has given them annual evaluations that are unrealistic and inflated. (Many studies have shown that principals' evaluations of teachers are far off the mark; their evaluations show absolutely no relationship to real teacher effectiveness as measured by student gains in achievement.) This is easy to do because the principal may be required by the teachers' union contract to give advance notice to teachers before he visits their classrooms; thus, the principal may have no idea of what really occurs daily in the classroom. It is part of the principal's job description to supervise teachers in the classrooms, but very few principals actually do this.

The principal has a boss at the school district headquarters, and someday he would like to be a boss at headquarters. The principal wants to show the boss that he can run his school competently with minimal supervision. That means that he is motivated to solve his problems within the school and not let complaints reach the people at headquarters.

The perceptive parent may think, "Aha! That means the principal will give in if I threaten to go over her head!" Unfortunately, that is not the case. School districts don't really care what parents want, especially if they are chronic complainers (i.e., any parent who complains more than once). The principal knows that the school district will back him up against a troublemaking parent, especially if the parent has not documented her case carefully. No, the desire to keep problems within the school actually works against the parent. The principal's motive is to keep the teachers happy. If a parent complains to the school district, the complaint drops like a pebble in the ocean, whereas if a teacher complains to the district, that could really rock the boat. The principal doesn't want the school district to think that he has personnel problems at the school that are impairing his ability to manage the school.

The principal is the "headmaster" or "head teacher" of the school. As such, he is responsible for teacher morale and enthusiasm. These teachers are tenured, so the principal knows they are going to be around long after Johnny is a fading yearbook photo. He must defend the teachers, right or wrong, so that other teachers know that they will be defended, too. Bastions of ignorance aren't bastions for nothing.

You, as a parent, can expect the principal to defend the teacher actively by offering you no information at all about a teacher's background, qualifications, prior assignments, or anything else. He will not share with parents any information about previous complaints or official job ratings. The principal will deny that any information about the teacher is relevant to the problem, even long after you have concluded that the teacher is the problem. The principal will actively try to shift the focus of the problem away from the teacher and onto your child.

You can also expect the principal to defend the teachers passively. The principal will never agree with any of your documented criticism of the teacher; he will not acknowledge the validity of the criticism, and may not even acknowledge that evil was spoken. In defending the teachers, he has to deny the existence of a problem, and ignore the reality of your needs.

In his efforts to protect the status quo, the principal may also attempt to deny the reality of the situation.

Clearly the principal is not going to join you in attacking the teacher. That would decrease his effectiveness in managing his staff. There is nothing to be gained by forcing a principal into a corner where he has to defend an incompetent teacher. A parent's attacking an incompetent teacher may be the "right" thing to do, because it is an attempt to have the teacher fired, thereby securing the greatest good for the greatest number of children. But it is an attempt doomed to failure, and it is not an effective approach to saving your own child. Remember that your child has no other advocate but you, and that you are the only hope in saving your child from that teacher. To do that, you need the principal's cooperation, not a confrontation.

By the time problems have reached the point that you feel compelled to go over the teacher's head to the principal, the emotional heat may have reached the boiling point. After all, you have already tried unsuccessfully to work things out with the teacher, which has been frustrating. And you feel that your child's future is being jeopardized—and that's scary.

To control your emotions at this emotional time, you need to consider what your child actually needs. It would not be helpful for you to "tell on" the teacher and then leave Billy marooned in that classroom. Before you go to the principal, you should consider the impact on the teacher. You should decide whether to inform the teacher, before the fact, that you will be going over her head. In any case, whether the teacher finds out beforehand from you or afterward from the principal, the teacher may not be happy. She may harbor a grudge against you (or your child) for harming her reputation with her boss. In extreme cases, she may even act out her resentment against your child. In less obvious ways, she may do what is required for your child, but she will do the absolute minimum. She may eliminate other areas where she might have been helpful to your child. Before you go over the teacher's head, you need to consider these possible side effects of your action.

It is also not helpful to your child for you to make unreasonable demands, raise your voice, threaten to go to the board or to your lawyer, or be swept away by the anger of the moment. Keep in mind that your child will be best served by reasoned discussion that focuses on the child's needs. If you want to succeed with the principal, you had better be prepared in four different ways.

1. You must be able to show that you tried to work with the teacher to solve the problem. If you have not done that, the principal will throw the problem back into the teacher's lap. You must show that you tried and failed to solve the problem at the classroom level. And of course, you *have* done all that, following the advice in Chapter 7.

2. To get the principal's approval, you will need to avoid confrontation and get her cooperation. In order to do that, you should try to be mindful of her background and the pressures that she faces daily.

3. You must show that you have done your homework: When you go to the principal, it isn't enough to tell him the problem and expect him to solve it. You must be prepared to describe the problem and its ramifications, suggest alternative solutions, and explain why your solution is the best available choice. In other words, you

should go into your meeting with your plans and goals already formulated.

4. You must be prepared to support your requests with documented evidence and observations, rather than with personal opinions.

Identifying and Achieving Your Goals

When you go to the principal, what will you ask for?

Some parents' needs are clear-cut. These mothers and fathers know they want to move their child out of the reach of a teacher who is abusive or generally incompetent.

But what if your child has a teacher like Mr. Hart? Mr. Hart is almost everything you could ask for in a fourth grade teacher—he is patient, enthusiastic, and intelligent. The children are fascinated by his science lessons, and because Mr. Hart's enthusiasm is contagious, they can't help becoming enthusiastic about school and about learning. The only problem is that Mr. Hart doesn't like math, so he doesn't teach it very often. Consequently, his students move on to fifth grade with poor skills in multiplication and long division, and with no introduction to the concepts of fractions and decimals. As a parent, you value the rare and good things that Mr. Hart brings to your child, so you don't want your child transferred out of his class; but you want the principal to push Mr. Hart to do his job in math or make some other arrangement to provide math instruction for your child and his classmates.

What do you ask for, if transferring your child is not a viable option? Sometimes your options are limited by the nature of the school. There are small schools with only one classroom per grade, so there is no other class for your child to transfer into. There are schools with more than one class per grade, but the class assignments are based on a tracking system; if your child were to transfer, he would move into a class with students far above or far below his skill and experience level. In fact, in any school that uses some criterion (non-English speaking, reading level, whatever) to assign students to classes, the assumption is that your child has already been assigned to the class that is best for him. Any transfer would put him in a class that is less appropriate for him. You need to consider whether the current situation is so bad that you are unable to work within the school's limitations, and whether a new situation would really be better.

Even in the smallest, most limited schools, there are options other than changing classrooms, and you should give them some thought—first, because you may like the alternatives, and second, because the principal will almost surely suggest them and you must be prepared to accept or reject these proposals.

Among the alternatives are supplementary programs to fill in the teacher's weak areas. Under this plan, the weak teacher is supported by extra aides and/or a mentor teacher who can supply expertise in the areas where the classroom teacher is inadequate. The same effect can be achieved by changing the class schedule to allow more time for weak areas or more time with other teachers. Team teaching and task swapping are also options in the case of a weak teacher.

If there really is a mismatch between student and teacher, the principal is more likely to allow a transfer. When the principal knows he has a bad teacher, he is much more likely to suggest one of these alternatives. That is because he knows he can't move the entire class to other teachers in other classrooms, and he can't move just a few, either. Furthermore, in order to maintain equal class sizes, each transfer requires a reciprocal transfer of some other child into the bad teacher's classroom; and the principal can already imagine the howls of protest about that. So the principal will try to keep the parents happy by finding ways to improve the education while keeping the bad teacher in place.

Before you meet with the principal, you should have a clear idea of which outcomes you are prepared to accept. The principal may have some other outcomes in his mind, so you should also know what other alternatives are possible. When you reach a compromise with the principal, you want to be sure that your compromise will actually solve your child's problem, and not just serve to appease you.

Documentation

In a court of law, where the judge is not swayed by opinions and vague recollections but by hard facts and well-documented records, the winning side is generally the side with the most compelling evidence. The same thing is true in schools; the side with the best documentation will prevail. Unfortunately, as a parent, you start with an enormous built-in disadvantage.

The school has files full of records on your child, and on her teacher. It has reams of test scores that show whether the other children in the class are flourishing or failing; you have none. The school is also backed up by several thick volumes of the Education Code that you have not read and probably wouldn't understand, since it is written in educational jargon.

And if your goal is to get your child transferred, the school doesn't have to justify its inaction. They don't have to defend the placement of your child in one regular classroom rather than another, and they don't have to justify leaving him there. The burden of proof is on you, so you have to document your case, but they don't have to document theirs.

What is "documentation"? And what sort of documentation must a parent present to offset the imbalance of evidence? Documentation is a written and dated record of facts and observations. And in order to be considered credible, the documentation you collect should be as free of opinion as possible. Ideally, you will present the kind of documentation that illustrates your point of view all by itself, without any further editorial comment from you. For example:

THE SITUATION: You believe your daughter's teacher can't teach English because she doesn't know it well herself.

YOUR DOCUMENTATION: "Here is Sara's English homework paper for October 27. Notice the grammatical errors in Mrs. Thompson's comments." Or, "Here are all of Sara's papers for the month of October. Notice that there are letter grades but no comments anywhere."

THE SITUATION: Your son is upset by a teacher who yells at the kids in class.

YOUR DOCUMENTATION: "On October 12, October 20, October 26, and October 29, Mrs. Grantham yelled at the children. I have talked with the parents of Cathy Wheeler, Tom Weber, Danny Kahn, Jenny Flores, and others. All of the children were upset by her tone and volume, and none understood why the class was yelled at."

THE SITUATION: Your daughter is confused in class because she has had too many substitute teachers.

YOUR DOCUMENTATION: "Jennifer had substitute teachers on September 24 and on October 15 and 22. Those were all Mondays. . . ."

THE SITUATION: Your first-grader doesn't like school.

YOUR DOCUMENTATION: "On October 9, 3:15 P.M., Melissa came home and announced, 'I'm never going back there!' On October 12, 3:15 P.M., Melissa came home in tears and wouldn't say why. October 16, 8:20 A.M., Melissa asked if she had to go to school that morning. October 22, 8:20 A.M., Melissa was very cheerful about going to school. She said, 'It's Monday. Maybe Miss Danvers won't be there today.' "

THE SITUATION: You tried to discuss your child's difficulty with the teacher and found her unhelpful.

YOUR DOCUMENTATION: "On October 27 I had a conference with Mrs. Wilton. Here is a written record of the topics covered and her responses to each of our inquiries." Or even better, "Here is a tape recording of our conversation."

THE SITUATION: Jeff doesn't seem to be learning much in class.
YOUR DOCUMENTATION: "We observed the class on the morning of October 18. After the first five minutes, the children became inattentive and some began to wander around the classroom. The teacher worked with small groups, but the unsupervised groups did nothing in her absence. Discipline was sporadic and unpredictable." Or, "We have talked with the Jamesons, the Kerners, the Browns, and the Gonzales family, all of whom had children in Miss Peterson's class last year. They all agree that their children were not prepared for the next grade in math, compared to classmates who had other teachers last year. We are concerned that the same thing may be happening this year."

THE SITUATION: Your third-grader's teacher doesn't like your child.
YOUR DOCUMENTATION: "Here is a collection of Alyssa's work. You will note that there are only negative comments. There are no words of encouragement." Or "Alyssa's disciplinary record, in your office, has become worse this year. Has Alyssa changed, or is there some other explanation?"

Facts are always more effective than opinions, because they are harder for the principal to refute or ignore. And if you are dependent on opinions, get expert opinions; documentation from experts outside the school is very effective, particularly in cases where the principal seems prone to inaction. If an optometrist says Elisabeth should sit at the front of the class, chances are excellent that she will be moved there. If a licensed child psychologist says that continuing in Mrs. Portland's class would be damaging to Joshua's mental health, chances are excellent that he will be moved. The side with the best documentation will prevail, and written reports from experts make for very strong documentation.

The school and district have lots of documentation on their side, some of which may be used to refute you, and some that you will never see. Among these resources are:

1. The teacher's personnel file. Dating back to the time of her hiring, these records include college transcripts, results of job application tests, and the interviewer's ratings. It also includes records of further education and in-service training, performance evaluations by principals over the years, and salary history. It may also include complaints filed by other parents in previous years. You will never see this file, because the teacher has a right to privacy.

2. Other personnel files, to compare with the file of your child's current teacher. You will not see these, because other teachers also have a right to privacy. The district also has aggregated information on teacher ratings by school (average salary, average experience, average rating at time of hire, and so on); but you will never see that, either. The district will deny its existence, or claim it is for administrative use only.

3. Standardized test results by classroom. These scores can be used to compare the relative effectiveness of teachers in each classroom of the school. The principal has read this information and may even have analyzed it, but he will never share the information with you.

The school certainly has standardized test results for each grade level for the district as a whole. They also have scores by subject and grade for each school within the district. This is information that should be a matter of public record, because parents and others who fund the schools have a right to know how effectively those schools are functioning. But if this information became public, it would create too many problems of accountability. School officials don't want to be held accountable for their students' performance.

You will probably need a court order to get this information released to the public. School districts like to give report cards, but they don't like to get them.

In addition, there may be information pertinent to your case in your own child's file at the school office. Each child's file includes his attendance record, grades, and standardized test scores from the beginning of kindergarten. Many children have thin files containing only this minimal information. On the other hand, if the child isn't plain vanilla, the file may have more interesting information that might include:

1. Disciplinary records of infractions and punishments.
2. Teachers' descriptions of parent-teacher conferences.
3. Notes from parents to excuse absences.

4. Copies of communication from school to home about the child's behavior, academic performance, and so on.

5. Parent response to such communication.

6. Parent permission for special testing, counseling, or special placement within the school district.

7. Copies of the results of testing or counseling by school personnel.

8. Copies of reports of testing or counseling by professionals outside the school, including testing or counseling initiated by parents.

9. Reports of meetings with school personnel, or among school personnel, to discuss the child's status and placement.

Sometimes a file contains information that is damaging to the child. That information may be incorrect or out of date, or it may be accurate but prejudicial to the child. Many teachers draw their initial impression of the child from that file, so if a child has been flagged (fairly or unfairly), there is little chance for her to get a fresh start each September. The child's reputation not only precedes him, it drags along behind him like an anchor.

Parents should know that a Freedom of Information law, the Family Educational Rights and Privacy Act of 1974, gives them access to their child's file. And they have the right to examine and make copies of everything they find in that file.

School personnel are aware of this law, but they seldom encourage parents to exercise their rights. Some have even developed ways to evade the law because they don't want to share all their information with parents. They may not have the documentation to justify things they have done to a child, and they don't want parents to discover this. Principals and teachers who wish to escape the problems of full disclosure have been known to establish their own separate files with the intent of hiding their written opinions or other sensitive information about certain children.

If you look at the official school file on your child and find it surprisingly thin, ask the principal if there are any other files containing information about your child. It is possible (but unlikely) that the principal may say yes and provide you with the additional information.

It is also possible that the principal may say, "Yes, there is additional information, but it is in my personal files." This means that the principal thinks he is a magician who can label the information "personal" and thereby make it magically exempt from Freedom of Information laws. The principal is wrong. A parent has the right of access to her son or daughter's file, regardless of how the school wishes to label the file. That a file contains personal opinions and subjective judgments does not make it exempt from parental scrutiny.

A third possibility, and perhaps the most likely one, is that the principal will say, "No, there is no other information . . ." It may be that the principal has left the sentence unfinished ("There is no other information . . . that I wish to show you"). Or it may be that there really is no other information, but if a parent feels confrontational, he could ask the principal to sign a statement attesting that he is complying fully with the Freedom of Information laws and that no other information exists, including documents containing subjective judgments about his child. This approach would certainly compel the principal to turn over all relevant information, but it would forever foreclose any chance for getting his cooperation. Unless you are planning to transfer your child out of the school altogether, this approach is not your best course of action.

In the final analysis, documentation is the key element in your attempt to save your child. Without it, the principal has no compelling reason to upset the status quo, no reason to act upon your request, and no reason to fear a reprimand from his supervisors. Try to go over his head without documentation and he'll just tell his boss that you are a noisy troublemaker, and his boss will believe him. You will accomplish nothing, and your child will suffer.

Now consider what will happen if you approach the principal with a well-documented set of facts in hand. The principal may want to maintain the status quo, but she can't. She knows that you are prepared and that you are not going to give up. She knows that, if she doesn't deal with this problem now, you are going to keep pushing and that you may even go over her head. If she turns down your request, can she justify the decision to her boss? It's a question worth considering, especially if there's more information in your documents than she really wants her boss to know about. . . .

A school principal, like the captain of a ship, looks to avoid storms and find ports of calm. He hasn't the time or the will to fight every squall that blows his way. Show him calm water and he will go there, just so he can attend to other things that are more important to him. His instinct and training tell him to avoid any changes, so your documentation, persistence, and cooperation must persuade him that change (minor change, a change in your child's favor) is the best way to avoid the storms and keep the ship afloat.

9

The School System Defends the Line

Before World War II, the French were fearful of another round of German aggression, so they built three lines of forts on the French-German border. These lines were known collectively as the Maginot Line. When the Germans attacked in 1939, they did not waste time, energy, and ammunition attacking the heavily fortified line; they simply went around it.

The school system protects itself from invading outsiders with its own Maginot Line made up of three lines of defense: the principal's desk, the district superintendent's office, and the school board meeting room. Wise parents will not storm these lines of defense and force a bloody confrontation; nor will they need to. They'll find it much easier just to go around them.

Getting Around the School's Defenses

You are in the school office, waiting to meet with the principal. You are sure now that Johnny's school problems are the fault of the teacher, and you have collected enough documentation to support your position. You know that helping parents is not a very high priority on the principal's "to do list," but you know enough not to antagonize her. Now you need to get the principal's approval to move your child to another classroom.

Meanwhile, in the next room, the principal sits behind a big old desk with chipped veneer. She knows why you are there, and she considers what her response to you might be. You are not the first family that has complained about Mrs. Duplin, and she knows that your complaints are justified, but she will never acknowledge it. She considers what could happen if she agrees to move your child; will she be flooded with requests from the parents of Mrs. Duplin's other students, wanting the same treatment? Will parents throughout the school begin asking for transfers at the first sign of trouble? How much disruption could this cause? Is it worth all the disruption just to help this one family? After all, families are concerned only with their one child, and the principal is responsible for so many. . . .

When the meeting begins, the principal has her defenses at the ready. She has used them many times before, and she is confident of their effectiveness. Following are the mainstays of the principal's arsenal.

DELAY

The principal knows that time is his greatest ally. Parents may feel great concern about a child's difficulties, but children have good days and bad days. The good school days make it hard for a parent to maintain great concern long enough to follow through on it. If the principal can stall for a while, there is a good chance the parents will cool off and let the problem slide. Or the parents will decide they "can't fight city hall" and give up entirely. Even if the parents do pursue the problem, the principal might be able to stall until the end of the year, at which time the problem "solves" itself.

How can you tell if the principal is using a delaying tactic? He will listen politely to your comments and then insist that he needs some time to gather more information. He will say that he wants to discuss the problem with the teacher, to observe the child in the classroom, or to consider alternatives that would best serve the child. These are reasonable requests; you can't expect a school administrator to make a good decision without looking at the facts from all sides. But the stalling principal will let as much time go by as possible. Your best plan, therefore, is to schedule a date for the second meeting before you have left the first meeting; if you don't, the delaying tactic will already be working effectively against you.

At the second meeting, the delaying principal will have gathered her information, but her report to you will be ambiguous. She cannot acknowledge the obvious conclusion, that the teacher is incompetent, so she pretends that the information itself is ambiguous. This gives her the opportunity to suggest some changes in the *child's* behavior or attitudes to cope with this situation, and then suggest that everyone allow enough time for the changes to show some effect. This is pure stalling, and both sides know it. The principal has not acknowledged that the teacher is the problem. Since her "solution" doesn't address the real problem, it has no chance of success. Agreeing to this is agreeing to help the principal ignore the problem of teacher incompetence.

I have even met principals so desperate to delay, they actually used the old auto salesman's standby: "I have a solution in mind, but I need to run it past my boss. It involves requesting an exception to our district policies. Give me a little time to discuss this further."

As time goes by, the principal does little, except to hope that you will give up the hunt. Most parents do.

TEACHER CONFERENCE

The principal who suggests involving the teacher in his conference with you is unwilling to confront unpleasant situations, and he has found that most parents feel the same way. He has discovered that a good way to defuse parents who are complaining about a teacher is to require them to voice their complaints in a face-to-face situation. Most parents will back off, too embarrassed to make their complaints in front of someone who might refute them. End of problem, school wins again, child loses.

There are two reasons why you should not be intimidated by this maneuver. First, your child is too important for you to give in easily; you are the child's only advocate and his last line of defense. Second, you have already learned not to attack the teacher. No matter how incompetent the teacher, you are not asking the principal to acknowledge teacher incompetence, because you know he can't and he won't.

Your argument is that there is a mismatch between your child and that particular teacher, and that the child should be transferred for the good of all concerned. This is an argument that can be made gracefully, regardless of the presence or absence of the incompetent teacher.

SHIFT THE BLAME

It is not very productive to drive a child to anger or depression, and then blame him for being angry or depressed. But that is what schools do. Bad teachers do this, and then principals back them up. The teacher may be malicious or incompetent, but that only becomes known after the children react to her malice or incompetence. It is common for children to react with hostility, frustration, boredom, or some other unacceptable behavior. Then, when parents complain about the teacher, the principal responds by blaming the children for their poor behavior.

Clearly, the principal who relies on this defense is focusing on the symptoms and ignoring the disease. She is also taking advantage of the fact that the child is young, small, inarticulate, and unable to fend off unfair accusations. Shifting the blame onto a child's shoulders is the work of a bully. It is, perhaps consequently, a technique more commonly used than parents may think. Before parents meet with the principal to request a transfer, they should anticipate the tactic of shifting the blame. Parents had better be very sure, before the meeting, that their child is not the cause of the problem, and they had better have documentation to support their conclusion. It is a sure bet that, during the meeting, the principal will point to the child's lack of achievement, or poor behavior, or whatever, and blame the child or the parent.

Parents should also be aware that the "blame-the-child" tactic can be very subtle. It is possible that the principal will never actually point the finger or lay the blame anywhere. Instead, he will suggest that the "troubled" child meet with the school counselor, or see the school psychologist, or seek outside tutoring to alleviate the classroom situation. These sound like constructive suggestions, and in some situations they are. But be sure to notice in them the implicit assumption that there is something lacking in the child, and that it is the child who needs to be "fixed." Is he being referred to counseling because he "seems too sensitive to criticism"? Or because he "has problems dealing with authority figures"? These may be indications that the school is blaming the victim.

Parents should ask *why* the child should be referred to a counselor or psychologist; they should question the unspoken assumption that the child is the problem. Is the school referring him to counseling because he is a rotten kid who needs help? Or is the school recommending counseling to help him cope with a rotten situation? Wouldn't it be simpler to change the rotten situation? What about the possibility that the teacher is at fault? Will the principal at least inquire into that possibility? Maybe it is the teacher who needs "fixing."

A referral to a counselor could be more than an opportunity to blame the child; it can also be a delaying tactic as well. Before you agree to counseling, make sure you aren't just sacrificing your child to another time-wasting excuse for doing nothing. Ask what the outcomes of such counseling might be. Often the school has no particular outcome in mind. They just think that he "needs" counseling, and the counseling becomes an end in itself. Counseling is treated as a solution to the problem, although at best it can only point to a solution.

Far too often the intent of counseling is to modify the child's behavior. For a child stuck in a class with a bad teacher, modifying her behavior means training her to accept the evil that is being done to her and to live quietly under oppression. If that is what the school wants, reject it, because the cure is worse than the disease.

It is important to know that sometimes school administrators recommend counseling because they are very serious about making a case against a particular child. The school counselor and school psychologist are considered to be "experts" whose opinions carry more weight than a parent's opinion. If a principal knows he will reject your request, but will have to justify that decision to his boss, he will call in the counselor or psychologist to back him up. On-staff therapists may be good at helping kids, but they may also be good team players, good at maintaining the status quo, and good at keeping their eye on the next rung of the career ladder in the school district.

Can parents refuse counseling for their child? Not really. Parents who refuse such intervention are labeled "uncooperative," which means that the school can neatly absolve itself of further responsibility for the child. What parents need, before they make the major commitment to allow counseling for their child, is a matching commitment from the school. Parents want the school to acknowledge that, if the problem is serious enough to warrant counseling, it is serious enough to warrant a classroom change . . . and the classroom change should be made at the start of counseling, not at some unspecified date in the nebulous future.

THE PRETTY BAUBLE

The principal has a big problem and she knows it. Yours is not the first complaint she has heard about Ms. Barton; it's not even the first one this year. She knows she has a bad teacher. She also knows it will take eighteen months' more documentation before the district can even think about filing a case for dismissal.

Where does one hide a bad teacher? This is the principal's quandary. In the past, there were staff positions where the principal could hide her worst teachers. The incompetent teacher could be assigned to "permanent substitute" or to "home teacher" working with temporarily and permanently bedridden students; but budget constraints have largely eliminated these positions. The central office has already filled its hiding places with other bad teachers, and second grade is already staffed. The library position has been cut back to part-time, so there's no place left to dump her.

What is worse, the principal can't move enough kids out of Ms. Barton's class to make everyone happy, and besides, she'd have to move some other poor child into the class, for each child she moves out. *You* might not be aware of it yet, but the principal is faced with a full-scale parent revolt, and she knows exactly when it will start— the morning after the parents all talk to each other at the open house (or other school function). The principal has to act now, and since she doesn't want to open a floodgate, the action won't be to transfer a child.

The principal's only option is to do something immediately to improve education in Ms. Barton's classroom. Barring that, she has to do something that *appears* to improve education there. She will offer you, and all the other unhappy parents, some pretty bauble to distract you and head off the coming revolt.

What kind of gem might you expect? The principal may assign more aide time to the class, or employ a student teacher or a mentor teacher to improve the student-teacher ratio in the classroom. She may enlist other, more talented teachers to team teach with Ms. Barton, or give her peer assistance in organizing and teaching the class. The principal might placate you by having teachers trade certain subjects, so that Ms. Barton no longer has to teach her weakest subject. Or, if Ms. Barton has been chronically absent, the principal might arrange for the class to have the same substitute consistently, so the children get some continuity. In a real pinch, the principal might even be able to divert a pair of new computers or other equipment into your child's classroom.

It is possible that you might be very pleased with these changes. They may be exactly what your child needs. Certainly, the principal has made a sincere effort to make things better. He hopes that you won't notice that your child is still spending a lot of time with the incompetent or destructive teacher. As a result of the changes, your child's education is better than it would have been otherwise, but it is still not as good as it should be. At this point, you must decide to grin and bear it or transfer out of the school. This school has already offered everything it has to offer.

STONEWALL

Some schools simply will not consider transfer requests. They insulate themselves behind bureaucratic policies and refuse all requests as "contrary to school policy." In such cases, the principal may listen politely (they are always polite) because many parents seek nothing more than a sympathetic ear; but then the principal will say no. He will offer his response diplomatically, and if he is the stalling type, may delay it for weeks, but it will still be a "no." Perhaps the rejection will be accompanied by excuses, and probably by "I hope you understand the school's position . . ." but it will still be a rejection.

Your child's problem has still not been solved. To solve it, you need to go over the principal's head, or transfer your child to another school. Either way, you will have to deal with school district headquarters.

The School District

Many parents, particularly disgruntled parents, think of the superintendent of schools as the last line of defense, the only ear available to them after the teacher and the principal have tuned them out. In some cases, the superintendent *can* be helpful. But it is best to approach the superintendent with a realistic and practical idea of what he or she can (or will) do for you.

If the superintendent in your town is typical, she came up through the ranks, first as a teacher, then as a principal. At one time, your superintendent probably looked forward to becoming a school administrator because of the power such a position entails. She thought that an ambitious person in this position of authority could do much to improve children's education. Once a superintendent assumes the mantle of power, she is often surprised to find out how little power an administrator actually wields over anything that happens at the child's level. The superintendent finds that she has limited control over the principals and even less control over teachers. Before long, the superintendent discovers that issues of curriculum and school policy are governed by the school board. At some point, the superintendent comes to realize that it is not her job to decide where the educational "train" will go; the superintendent's job is merely to keep the train running.

In fact, the superintendent is no longer an educator; he is a corporate manager hired by the school board. In fact, the skills that the school board expects from the superintendent have nothing to do with either teaching or learning. What the school board wants from an administrator is conservative day-to-day management of a large, financially critical enterprise. That requires good political and managerial skills, a knowledge of finance and budgeting, planning ability, and good public relations skills. If the superintendent is ever fired, his termination would have more to do with a lack of management or political skills than with any failure on the superintendent's part as an educator.

Consequently, the superintendent himself is unlikely to solve the problems of an individual student. The superintendent's day is tied up with lots of meetings, with board members, union officials, or administrative staff. The superintendent prepares for and attends school board meetings; he or she also may testify at legislative hearings, go to conferences, meet with community leaders and businessmen. In smaller districts, the superintendent may be involved in meetings and conferences with teachers, and occasionally may become involved in serious problems involving individual teachers and students. In larger districts, the superintendent has *no* contact with individual students and only occasional contact with individual teachers.

On the other hand, before you step into the superintendent's office, it may comfort you to understand that the person behind the desk is someone who loves children and chose a career in education to change and improve their lives. The superintendent's rise through the professional ranks from teacher to principal and beyond is often a bittersweet progression, especially for a real hands-on superintendent, because each step removes the administrator further from the children. But any such regret and frustration on behalf of the superintendent creates a real opportunity for a parent who approaches with the right message.

If the parent can get past the secretaries and the lower-level administrators and speak directly to the superintendent, that parent will likely find a receptive ear. The superintendent rarely has a chance to step in and make a positive difference in the life of an identifiable child; when presented with the opportunity, most superintendents will jump at the chance.

Getting Around the District's Defenses

Only in a small district can you expect to deal directly with the superintendent. In most districts, you will be dealing with a lower level administrator or even a clerk. These people may not share the superintendent's calling to improve the world; they may be petty bureaucrats who equate job security with their ability to follow every subparagraph of every regulation.

Most school districts have rules governing intradistrict transfers, conditions that allow a school to enroll a student who resides in another school's territory. Depending on the size of the district, they may have personnel specifically assigned to handle transfers within the district. And depending on enrollment capacities and racial balance requirements, they may be either rigid or flexible in their transfer policies. In fact, their regulations may vary in flexibility from year to year, or even within a school year. Many districts are much more generous in the first few weeks of a semester than at the end. It's easier to get a transfer if you are asking ahead of time for a change to occur at the beginning of the next semester.

Rules vary from district to district, and you should find out your district rules before you request a transfer. Some districts will happily allow working parents to enroll their children at the school nearest their work; others insist that you enroll them at the school nearest your home. Most districts will allow you to enroll your child at a school nearest your day-care provider, especially if you can provide compelling reasons why your day-care arrangements can't be changed. Cost, for example, may be a convincing reason. Transportation difficulties between home, school, and day care can also be a compelling reason for a district to offer some flexibility.

Some districts welcome enrollments from nonresidents, space permitting. A district may find it easier to justify nonresident enrollment for someone who owns property, operates a business, or is employed within its boundaries; this varies, depending on state regulations and district policies.

School districts can be wary of parents trying to sneak past their enrollment policies. Some districts will not tell you what the criteria are for approving a transfer, or they may not tell you which reasons are most likely to be successful this year. Since the district will give you only one trip to the batter's box, you need to make a hit on your first attempt. You may find it useful to talk to your child's principal first, before you go to the district; he may be so anxious to divest himself of your child's problem (and your complaints!) that he might be helpful in telling you which reasons are finding favor this year. If you have selected a school for your child because it has a particular program that addresses his problem, talk to that school's principal and try to enlist her help in getting the transfer. If your child has been having horrible peer problems, or is suffering from a serious mismatch with his current teacher, his current principal may be very helpful in getting him transferred out.

THE PING-PONG PLOY

Larger school districts discourage parents by means of a bureaucratic maze. It starts with your first phone call, which reaches a voice-mail system with many branches, none of which corresponds to your question. You are then sent shuttling through electronic purgatory, occasionally encountering a human voice who directs you to some other limbo.

Nor are you likely to fare any better if you visit the district office in person. There you bounce from office to office, directed again and again to yet another destination by bureaucrats who disclaim responsibility for your problem. You ricochet back and forth between the same offices like a Ping-Pong ball, filling out forms in one place and depositing them in another. Then you wait for action from a third office, which can't act until it gets authorization from a fourth place . . . and does anyone know where the forms are? They must have been misplaced. . . .

The district didn't design the bureaucratic maze to frustrate parents so they would give up, but that outcome doesn't upset them, either. Remember that service to the client is a low priority for a bureaucrat; it's much more important to follow procedures than to help the child.

If you find yourself caught between two bureaucratic agencies, each waiting for the other to do something, ask to see the boss. When you get bogged down with a lot of clerks and forms, ask to see the person who *can* make a decision, and appeal to her for help. She may cut through the red tape and solve your problem if only to save herself the time she'd waste helping you fill out forms.

THE HOT POTATO

Keep in mind that the superintendent's main task is management of her organization. It is futile to ask her to do anything that would disrupt the district or make her appear to be an ineffective manager. For example, you cannot ask her to overrule a direct order from your child's principal, because that would undermine the principal's authority and create resentment that would spill over into other areas and other issues. You cannot ask her to transfer a teacher, because that also creates too many ripples. You *can*, however, ask her to waive a district rule, if you can give her a good enough reason, and if it won't be followed by a flood of parents requesting the same waiver. And you can certainly ask her to allow the transfer of your child to another school within the district.

If your child's problem could be solved within the school (perhaps by changing his classroom), but the principal seems unwilling to resolve the problem, you have a dilemma: Should you ask the principal to help you get district approval of a transfer to another school? The principal may help you just to get you out of his hair; or he may oppose you from personal pique. You will have to judge, based on what you know of this individual, whether he would be willing to act on your behalf.

If you go to the district, asking the superintendent to force the principal to do something he could have done on his own, you are doomed to failure. You would be asking the superintendent to discard the smooth working relationship he has established with the principal, all for the sake of your unproved allegations. That won't happen. Worse, what *will* happen is that the superintendent will throw the problem back into the principal's lap like a hot potato, and you will be back where you started. Except now you will be facing a principal whom you have alienated.

Rather than ask the district to overrule the principal, find some other reason to ask for a transfer—cite transportation or day care, or access to special programs elsewhere. Remember, criticizing the principal to her boss is no more effective than criticizing the teacher to the principal, and for all the same reasons. If the principal really is ineffective, and the district knows it, then they must have reasons for doing nothing, or they would have acted already. If the principal is ineffective and the district *doesn't* know it, then they aren't about to discipline him on your word only. In either case, you are telling the superintendent something he doesn't want to hear . . . and the messenger in such cases is rarely rewarded.

So what should you do to avoid being treated like a hot potato? When you go to the district, know what you want and phrase it in a way that fits the district's goals. Then give them reasons why they should resolve the problem with a quick stroke of their pen rather than throw it back to the principal. It's easiest if you are asking for something, like a transfer, that only the district (not the principal) is authorized to do. Rather than criticize the school or its principal, cite a mismatch between the student and school. Indicate politely that the district can have "closure" if they will allow the transfer, but you will be coming back to them again and again if your child stays at the same school.

Taking Your Problem to the School Board

Each school district has a superintendent who makes most of the day-to-day decisions about managing the school district. The superintendent's freedom in decision making is limited by state and federal regulations that must be observed; and there are officials in the State Department of Education who have some responsibility to oversee her. Nevertheless, for the most part, the superintendent is the big boss within the organization, with a wide latitude of decision-making power. But the superintendent is not a dictator, ruling by divine right. She was hired by the school board and can be fired by the school board. She must report to the school board and obtain their continuing support. That is what makes the school board, or even a single sympathetic board member, such a valuable ally of the concerned parent.

The ultimate boss in a democracy is the will of the people. In the steps of the Founding Fathers, we have decided that an educated citizenry makes for a better democracy. So the people have agreed to earmark a certain amount of public money for the education of children, and the school board is the public's way to ensure that their education money is being spent wisely and effectively.

The school board, as the representative of the public will, sets the budgets and the policies for the schools in their district.

The board does not get involved in personnel decisions, such as the hiring and firing of teachers. Depending on the size of the district, they may be involved in the hiring of principals (in a small district, the choice of a principal does involve questions of policy). The board always plays a part in the hiring and firing of the superintendent, and sometimes also the hiring and firing of his top assistants. The school board does not micromanage; they do not get involved in the day-to-day decisions of running the school district; that's what they hired the superintendent to do.

The motivation of the board members is to provide quality education at an appropriate cost. School districts vary greatly in their definition of "quality" education, and they vary even more greatly in the level of quality that they are willing to pay for, although many states are removing that issue from the school boards by standardizing the funding level across all districts in the state.

Another significant motivation for school board members is reelection. In smaller districts, everyone knows something about the character of the schools and their strengths and weaknesses. Everyone has a friend on the school board or knows someone who does. In this ideal situation of a well-informed citizenry, the school board members are more likely to be reelected (or not) based on their record: Is the district delivering quality education at appropriate costs? Did the board set policies that represent what the people want? Have they succeeded in getting the superintendent to implement those policies? And most important, are their efforts reflected in the educational well-being of the community's children?

In larger districts, where voters are not so well informed, more sinister patterns are common. Board members try to assure reelection by pandering to certain groups that can get out the vote, and quality education sometimes takes a backseat to other considerations. Board members may appeal to certain interest groups by directing the school district to hire contractors or administrators only from that interest group. The interest group may be geographic, religious, ethnic, or other.

The best-organized interest group in large cities is the teachers' union. Teachers contribute generously and campaign hard for their favored candidates, those who are friendly to their union and who, quite often, are *members* of their union. In the absence of counterbalancing forces, the teachers' union can take over the district. This happened recently in Los Angeles; the new board's first action was to give a sweetheart contract to the union, one that nearly drove the school district into bankruptcy. On the brink of financial collapse, the district has had to take back part of the raises that were granted. This, in turn, has made Los Angeles teachers very angry. Now they work even harder to elect their own candidates. As a consequence, the school board members are more concerned with pleasing the union than with quality education or appropriate cost controls, and no one speaks for the parents or the public.

The balance of power between the superintendent and the board of education varies from district to district. But the board tends to be more directly involved in the daily operation of the district when:

- the district is small
- an experienced board has hired a young, inexperienced superintendent
- the new superintendent comes from outside the district
- a new board majority emerges from a contested election

A superintendent is more likely to have the strength to resist board meddling and micromanaging if she is older, more experienced, in a larger district, and/or has a power base of her own among the people.

Getting Around the School Board's Defenses

You should not take your problem to the school board in open meeting. That would be a certain way to offend everyone and to ensure that you won't get what you want. If you go to the school board at all, I recommend that you take your problem to an individual school board member, to his school district office if he has one, or to his business office. You will get a more sympathetic ear if you do not phone the board member at home during the evening.

The board member may help you, but if he doesn't, the reason is usually this: IT'S NOT HIS JOB. The school board generally does not and certainly *should* not get involved in the problems of individual students, conflicts between students and teachers, or even personnel problems at a particular school. The board would be undercutting the school's administrators if it meddled in the day-to-day operation of the schools.

But the school board will take up a worthy cause if you can convince them that it is their obligation to get involved. They will throw the problem back to the district unless you can give them good reasons not to do so. Some effective arguments you might use to enlist the board's support are:

• You have already gone through all of the correct channels and nothing has been done to alleviate your child's difficulty. In other words, the school acknowledges what the problem is, and the solution is within district policy, but the school won't act in the student's behalf, and the district is unwilling to force it to. You need the board to lean on somebody, to make them do what their own policies say they should do.

• You have gone through the appropriate channels and got trapped in the Ping-Pong Ploy. Instead of taking responsibility for your child's problem, the various district departments are pointing at each other and saying, "Not my problem, it's your problem." You can't find anyone in the school district administration with the power (or the will) to solve a simple problem. You need the board to compel *someone* to take ownership of the problem.

• The problem is not just a problem with your child, it is a wider concern that involves an entire class, an entire school, or the entire district. For example, your child's test scores may indicate a weak curriculum rather than a weak student. Or your child's school has insufficient resources compared to other schools in the district. The school district's failure to solve a problem of this nature reflects widespread mismanagement at the school or district level. And you can prove it, or at least cite other examples of the same type of mismanagement. You need

the board to fulfill its obligation to oversee the effective
management of the school district.

Board members are elected officials, and if they take
their positions seriously, they will do what they can to
maintain the goodwill of the people who elected them.
"Constituent relations" is the term for all the little services that elected officials provide just to keep the voters
happy. There may be things the board members can do
for you, in the name of constituent relations . . . but only
if they like you well enough to want to help you. So be
pleasant and cooperative.

Never storm the school board and threaten mass action or a parent revolt. That will only provoke resistance
and consign your cause to doom. If your argument is good
enough to rally the masses, it should be good enough to
enlist board support without public outcry. Board members are savvy enough to sense which way the political
winds are blowing, long before they hear crowds shout-
ing outside their doors.

Remember, there are official lines of power that show
up on the district's organization charts, and along those
lines, the board keeps its nose out of the district's daily
operation. But there are also unofficial, invisible lines of
communication and power that don't show up on any-
body's organization charts. Board members and school
officials may have worked together, played together,
coached Little League together. A board member may be
able to call the principal and say, "Joe, I had a concerned
parent in my office today. A nice woman. She has a problem that you can solve. Will you try to make her happy?"
The principal who was never interested in helping you
might be eager to comply with a board member's request.

The principal's reaction could variously be described as a smart political move or as favoritism; you don't care, because it accomplishes your goal in a way that would not have been possible if you'd acted alone.

Sometimes you won't find a solution for your child's problem at the school level or the district level. Maybe all of the public school personnel are unwilling to help your child, or maybe they are simply incapable. There are certain students, certain situations, certain needs that call for a solution outside the public school milieu. Once you have exhausted or rejected the offerings of the public schools, it's time to look at other options.

PART THREE

PRIVATE SCHOOLS

AND

PERSONAL

SOLUTIONS

10

Private Schools

"I felt that my daughter, Martha, had needs that weren't being met in public school, so I moved her into a smaller, private school," said the mother of a third-grader. *"Now I pay $8,000 a year tuition and her needs are still not being met."*

There are many reasons families may choose to have their children educated in places other than government-run schools. Some feel, as Martha's mother did, that a private school can offer its students more personalized instruction. Others feel that the private schools offer a more protected environment from the harsh realities of the world; and others may be looking for more advanced work for their children. These parents choose, sometimes after a brief experience with public schools, to enroll their children in private schools (either independent schools or religious schools).

Transferring a child to a private school is not a decision parents take lightly. Private schools can be pricey—and most elementary school children are hesitant to leave a school to which they have become accustomed. These factors are enough to give most parents pause. Still, many well-intentioned mothers and fathers make the leap into private education on their children's behalf without really knowing what private schools offer—and what they do not.

Many parents don't know that schools that do not accept government funding are also free from most government regulations. The thousands of pages of the State Education Code do not apply, for the most part, to private schools, although laws vary from state to state. Private schools are free to decide their own philosophy, organization, and curriculum. They choose their own textbooks. They can also select students on any basis they wish, including religion (but probably not including race), and they are free to "select out" students who don't "fit into their program." Private school administrators are free to hire whatever teachers they like, including (in most states) teachers who do not hold state-issued credentials or certification. In many states, the only government regulations that apply to private schools are the health, safety, and zoning regulations that apply to any building of equivalent size, use, and location.

You may have a child in a public school who needs to escape from a bad teacher, and you are thinking of private school as an option. Or you may have a child already enrolled in a private school, with a bad teacher, and you are wondering what your options are. In either case, you need to know more about private schools and what you can do to make your child's educational experience more fulfilling.

Why Private Schooling?

Your local public school, by law, must accept children from the entire range of abilities and demographics: the geniuses and the intellectually slow, the fit and the physically challenged, the rich and the poor, the eloquent and the non-English speaker. They come to your school from shacks and mansions, from all parts of the globe, bringing their culture and their customs with them. It is the task of the public school to educate them all with some degree of equity, and that can be a very difficult task. In a time of too little money and too many goals, the public school may not be succeeding in providing the education parents want for their children.

In response to difficult times like these, parents may look to private schools to deliver what they consider to be "quality education." And the qualities that many of them are seeking are these: selective student body, smaller classes, and better values.

Selective Student Body Achievement-oriented private schools get many more applicants than they have spaces to offer, so they can be very selective about whom they admit. Using a rigorous testing process, they screen out the low achievers and any applicants with academic or social problems, then make up their classes of bright and capable youngsters handpicked from the upper half of the range of abilities. The competitive selection process, administrators believe, enables each class to progress faster, because the students need not wait around for slower classmates to comprehend each new concept. The selective school can then proceed with an advanced curriculum, one that uses materials appropriate for the bright students and focuses more on concepts and has less drill work. If you have a child bright enough to gain admittance, this could be a good school choice for your family.

A well-known story in educational circles, possibly true, illustrates another "benefit" of selective schooling. A study was done of the prestigious Harvard Business School, in which graduates were compared to people who had been admitted to the Harvard program but had never attended. The surprising results were that there was no significant difference between the two groups. The message of the study is that the benefit of any prestigious school may not be in the education they actually provide, but in the admissions process that stamps the admittee as "prime stock." There are many fine secondary schools that admit only bright children; at the end of four or six years, most of them are still smart enough to get into good colleges . . . but maybe not because of the education they received. Maybe they were first-rate kids who would have succeeded anywhere, and the only "value added" by the school was the label it put on the package.

Smaller Classes Typical class size in a private school is about twenty, give or take a few students—many fewer than in most public schools. And since the students are more homogeneous in ability (children at the low end of the range were never admitted), the teacher's attention is less fractionalized. It is much harder for a child to get away with bad behavior in a smaller class; and it's harder for a child to fall through the cracks and go unnoticed when he doesn't understand something. The teacher should be able to give more time and attention to each child in a private school. If your child works better with a more personal relationship, then a private school may benefit him.

Better Values Where does a child acquire his attitudes, values, and beliefs? The preschooler gets almost all of his values from his parents. But as he progresses through elementary school, he gradually acquires more and more of his values from nonfamily influences. By the time he begins junior high school, he has already absorbed from his parents about all that he is going to get, in terms of attitudes, values, and beliefs. At this stage, the child is transferring his loyalties from his first role models—his parents—and adopts the attitudes, values, and beliefs of his peers. Recognizing this rite of passage, many parents opt for a private school in the hope that their child's peer group will be made up of kids who share the family's positive values. Parents want their child to be among others who have books at home, who care about the quality of their homework, who invest time and effort in endeavors (like education) that won't pay off for years to come or may pay off in nonmonetary ways, and who strive for excellence and self-improvement. They value the school for its ability to mold its student body, by example and peer pressure, into a group of young adults with good values, attitudes, and beliefs. They know that if the values are there, the mastery of facts and content will follow naturally.

Can parents have these values reinforced at the local public school? Of course they can. The public school has all kinds of children, including children with the right values and attitudes. Depending on the school, there may also be children with low ambition and low standards of conduct. Each parent must observe whether his child habitually falls in with good kids or bad kids, and then decide whether his child will gravitate toward the right peer group in the public school.

The Coleman Study, a massive study by the U.S. Office of Education, asked why some schools are better than others. It concluded that 85 percent of the variance in school quality is due to the difference in the students. Only a tiny fraction of the variance is due to differences in the teachers, administrators, library, physical plant, and everything else. So, according to this study, the quality of a school is largely determined by the quality of its students. Private schools think they set themselves apart from other schools by differences in their mission statements and philosophies. The truth is that those mission statements may attract certain kinds of families and certain kinds of students. Ultimately it is the school's students, and not the mission statement itself, that sets the tone for the school.

But what happens when a child is struggling in a private school? As one parent said, "I'd love to take him out. But now his friends are there, his social life is there, and his only school experience is there. He may be unhappy, but he doesn't want to leave." Almost every child will choose to keep the familiar demons he knows, rather than trade for a set of demons unknown. And many private school children take pride in their school; they like the idea that they are playing in the big league, the best school in town. To such a child, leaving his school would be moving down to the minors. And the problem may be compounded by the parents, who enjoy having their child stamped "prime stock" by his enrollment in the private school, and who would suffer a loss of image if their child can't make it there. Nevertheless, if the child is unhappy or unsuccessful, at some point the parents need to ask themselves, "Is this the right choice for our child at this time?"

Why Not Private Schooling?

Here's a comment from a working-class parent whose son is having reading difficulties at an expensive, competitive private school. "I meet parents at fund-raisers and school functions and all they talk about is academic excellence and achievement. I want to tell them that, despite the school's reputation, my son is having real difficulty. I want to know if their children are having problems with the same teachers I'm having problems with. But I don't dare. I don't even dare enroll my son in the peer tutorial program. I feel that it will cast aspersions on my son—like he's not good enough to be there."

Private schools can be very competitive, and parent egos can become so caught up in the competition that they cannot bring themselves to discuss their children's struggles. Parents are expected to act as cheerleaders for the "extraordinary educational experience" that is being bestowed on their children—whether that educational experience is really extraordinary or not. Those parents who do gripe are thought to be disgruntled or disloyal; they aren't the ones called on to join committees and become part of the "in group." They become isolated from the movers and shakers, and it's hard for isolated parents to create a groundswell of complaint against any real problem (like a bad teacher).

Private schools have many of the same problems that public schools have, plus a few that are unique. In fact, each of the reasons for choosing private schooling has a dark side that offers a corresponding reason *not* to choose private schooling.

Selective Student Body It's great for the ego to qualify as part of a very selective student body; it's not so great when your child is selected out, particularly if he is forced out midway through his education. I know of one small private high school that proudly graduates a dozen students per year, all of whom go to prestigious Ivy League colleges; but they start with sixty students in the seventh grade and drop 20 percent of them each year. This school does a fine job for the twelve survivors, but it is destructive to the other forty-eight.

The selective student body also tends to be homogeneous in its ethnic and socioeconomic mix. Children may not be preparing for the real world when they are educated within a limited stratum of society. Many elementary school parents say, "That's fine with me, if my kids are exposed only to other kids who share my values." But many other parents think this leads to a limited worldview, and to weak skills in dealing with people who are different from oneself.

Smaller Classes If a school's most attractive feature is its smaller classes, it may be attracting children who desperately need the closer attention and tighter control that small classes offer. The school may be weighted with children who could not succeed in the large classrooms of the public school; their parents sent them here in hopes that smaller classes would solve all of their educational and social problems.

Moreover, if the private school classes are smaller, the school itself may be smaller, too. Many private schools offer only one class per grade. If your child is incompatible with the teacher of that grade, your options are very limited; you may not be able to solve the problem within that school. And you may not want to walk away from the tuition you paid up front. . . .

Better Values You want your child to strive for excellence and to care about the quality of his work, but the quest for achievement can get out of hand. Some schools set such high standards of quality that kids can't possibly meet the requirements and are therefore made to feel like failures, even when they are doing work that would be exceptional in a normal school. Or the school may set reasonable standards, but encourage the child to set such high expectations for himself that he is still doomed to failure. Any values that are estimable in moderation may become harmful in excess.

And there are other problems that occur more frequently in private schools.

Competition The top private school in Los Angeles gives a prize each year to each grade's Most Improved Student, and the school basks in the glory of having helped these children succeed. What the school doesn't know is that the winning child in each grade has been tutored extensively, expensively, and secretly; the success of these children has nothing to do with the school's efforts.

Parents want their child to succeed, even to excel in the school. They tried to give their child an extra edge in life by giving him this private school education, and now they are trying to give him an extra edge within the private school, so they get a tutor. And they don't tell the other parents, because they want their child to appear effortlessly superior. And the other parents do the same thing. Very soon, the few kids who don't have their own private tutors are at a disadvantage.

When the private tutor is so common that it is no longer an edge, the really competitive parents go to greater lengths. A southern California company offers to prepare your child for standardized tests *by using the exact tests he will be taking!* And they are doing a brisk business among competitive parents for whom ethics are irrelevant.

Lack of Special Education Programs Private schools do not offer special education programs. They expect that the admissions office will screen out any children with learning problems. When a learning disability sneaks through the selection process, or develops in someone already at the school, the private school is unprepared. They don't have the materials or the specialists to diagnose or deal with such a difficulty. Many have no interest in helping serious problems, particularly if the struggling student is likely to pull down the class average on standardized tests. The typical private school response to a child's mild learning difficulty is "Get a tutor," and the typical response to a child's serious problem is "Find another school." They simply aren't equipped or inclined to deal with learning disabilities. They think that's what the public schools are for.

Secrecy A parent was concerned because his child was struggling in his private school class. The parent spoke to other parents to see if the problem was widespread and if it had been continuing over several years. Soon the parent was called into the office of the headmaster, who accused the parent of "disrupting the school's morale." The headmaster offered the parents a choice of stopping their inquiry or leaving the school. They stopped the inquiry. Schools that are very selective and have long waiting lists can be as arbitrary as any maître d' at a trendy restaurant. And parents hate to give up that "prime stock" certification.

Arrogance Some private schools, particularly those that pride themselves on their stratospheric test scores, have adopted the attitude, "We know everything about education and you parents know nothing. So give us your child, give us your money, and now shut up." If a parent has a suggestion or just a question, the response is, "This is the way we do it here. This is how we have always done it here. Our methods have worked in the past, and we have no desire to change. Change would mean lowering our standards." It's hard to argue with success, and a school can get away with this arrogant attitude if they have a record of success. But it's an attitude that doesn't leave much room for individual differences. The child must either fit the mold, or leave and make room for another crisply cut cookie who *will* fit the mold.

Bad Teachers There is a dirty little secret that parents don't expect to find when they are paying $10,000 a year: Private schools have bad teachers, too.

The Bad Teacher in the Great School

You have found the right school for your child. It has challenged and excited her and helped her grow intellectually, socially, and ethically. She has come to practice the habits of honesty, courtesy, and hard work. You have

been pleased with the school and its effect on your child
. . . right up to the beginning of this school year.

This year, your child is the same and the school is the
same, but something is out of tune. Is the teacher a bit
off-key? Can it be that this wonderful school has a bad
teacher?

Yes, it is very possible. Public schools do not have a
monopoly; bad teachers can appear in all kinds of school
settings. Private school teachers cover the full range of
ability, from excellent to execrable.

But private school teachers are different from public
school teachers in several ways.

Less Pay Except for the very top private secondary
schools, the pay scales for private school personnel is
much lower—about 70 percent of public school wages.
This comes as a surprise to most parents, who think the
private schools pay *more*. After all, the tuition at a private
school is thousands of dollars, and the public school tuition is zero. But parents forget that private schools pay
salaries out of tuition money *instead of* tax money, not *in
addition to* tax money.

If private school teachers are paid less, does it mean
that these teachers are inferior? Not necessarily. Often it
means they are motivated by nonfinancial concerns. They
may prefer the carefully controlled working conditions
(compared to public school teaching): fewer kids, better-
behaved kids with no serious problems, a school located
in a nice neighborhood, and less bureaucracy. The teacher
may be a parent herself, and prefer the hours that coincide with her child's daily schedule and vacation schedule. The teacher may even be a parent of a student
enrolled at that school. The elementary private school

teacher is usually not the primary breadwinner in the family; more often, the spouse is a doctor, lawyer, or businessperson, and the teacher's income is very secondary, used for discretionary spending like vacations and long-term savings. One cannot get married and raise a family on a private school teacher's salary, and few people try.

Public school pay scales are usually published documents, with wages based on experience and education level. Private school pay scales, on the other hand, are never published and are much more flexible. Private school pay is negotiated individually and merit *is* often a factor. Teachers who take on more responsibility are usually paid more.

Benefit packages are much smaller in private schools, particularly where many teachers are not the family's primary wage earner. Those schools assume that the teacher's spouse will provide retirement and medical plans, so they provide less in those areas. In schools where medical, retirement, dental, and other benefit plans are available, they may be offered as part of a "smorgasbord" in which the teacher chooses among the benefits she wants. Usually these benefits are funded by employees rather than employers—more benefits, smaller paycheck. Private school benefits may be meager, but they are an improvement over the standard private school benefit plans of the past, which were zero.

Less Training The typical public school teacher went to a state college, maybe majored in education, and has had teacher training leading to a credential.

My observation of the typical private school teacher is that he or she was more likely to have gone to a private

college or a more prestigious state university and majored
in a liberal arts field. The teacher never took education
classes, and never bothered with credential programs,
and has had no formal training in classroom management, but in a private school such training is less critical
than for the public school counterparts. The teacher simply doesn't have the same classroom management problems. On the other hand, the private school teacher may
have a higher verbal IQ and a better command of the subject matter. Having specialized in a particular subject
rather than "education" compensates for the teacher's
lack of teacher training.

Different Goals The public school teacher enters the
profession intending to make a career of it, and expecting
the wages to be fair for that kind of work. He stays in
teaching either for the love of it or because he lacks alternatives. In private schools, many teachers come in expecting to teach for only a few years: until they decide
which graduate school to attend, until the kids are in high
school, until the student loan is paid off, or (in Los
Angeles) until the screenplay sells. They stay because
they like the life; the pay is rotten but the work's not
hard. The vacations are great, and they always coincide
with their own child's vacation. The working conditions
are good. They have more autonomy within their classroom and don't have a boss breathing down their necks
all the time. And the private school setting allows them
the satisfaction of watching children grow over a long
period of time, unlike public school with its high tran-
siency rate, where the class roll changes weekly.

　　When a private school teacher wants a career in
teaching, she typically searches for a job among the

wealthy suburban school districts that offer conditions similar to the private schools, but with salaries and benefits that are much more generous.

Tenure Public school teachers obtain tenure, a lifetime contract, usually after three years of employment. After that, they cannot be fired for much less than a felony conviction. And if the school district runs out of money or has a decline in enrollment and has to cut back on teachers, seniority rules: The newly hired great teacher will be laid off and the tenured incompetent will be retained.

The private school never offers tenure; in fact, it rarely even offers a multiyear contract to any individual teacher. Almost all private school teachers are employed on a one-year contract running from September to August, with no assurance of employment beyond the contract's expiration. Furthermore, most contracts have clauses that allow the school to terminate the contract with two weeks' notice for cause, or one month's notice without cause. These clauses are rarely exercised, but in effect these clauses mean that private school teachers are working on month-to-month contracts.

Private school teachers are not protected by seniority. Their best job protection is simply to do a good job. Another protection is that if the school is a good one and if the local economy isn't depressed, there should be no fluctuations in enrollment, even when enrollment in the local public school is fluctuating. So there should be no need for layoffs, and employment should be secure for a good teacher.

Ethnicity Private school teachers are much more likely to be white, and the private school faculty will be less diverse—just like the student body. The better private schools, however, are trying very hard to become more diverse in both enrollment and employment.

Part-time Teachers For art, music, physical education, playground supervision, and foreign languages, many small schools turn to part-time staff. These teachers vary widely in quality. Some are excellent, but many are less committed to education, less committed to that school and its values, less understanding of children and of classroom management. They were hired more for availability than quality; pay scales for these noncore subjects are very low, even by private school standards.

Part-time teachers in a private school may be poorly qualified, poorly paid, and may have the mind-set of temporary workers. But you can't compare them to their counterparts in the public schools because, for these minor subjects, the public schools may not *have* any teachers.

Private schools may appear to be "immune" from the problems that haunt the public schools (some private schools invest a great deal of time and money to create the illusion of "immunity"), but that does not mean they are less likely to hire the same sorts of bad teachers, plus a few who are unique. There are many teachers who are well intentioned but untrained in diagnosing learning problems. Although their classes are smaller and each child gets more individual attention, the problems remain undiagnosed because the teacher has never learned what symptoms to look for. And the problems remain unsolved, because the teacher has not been trained to adjust to different learning styles and learning needs. Even if your expert points out a learning difficulty to the teacher, she doesn't know what materials or methods to use to accommodate the problem.

Another bad teacher common to public and private schools alike is the one I refer to as "the labeler." This teacher has watched your child over the years and has read his permanent file, so that she knows what to expect from him. The unfortunate side effect of this practice is that it never gives a child a fresh start. He can never turn over a new leaf; his reputation always precedes him, and he is always reacting to teacher perceptions based on the way he *used to be*.

Here are some other bad teachers more common in private schools.

Mr. Drake Mr. Drake can't choose between applying to business school and buckling down and getting a law degree, and he's too immature to face the business world, so he is taking a detour—a job at a good private school. He is clueless about what is a reasonable expectation of performance from elementary school children. He had heard that the children would rise to his expectations, so he should expect a lot. Consequently, he has set his standards so high the children cannot possibly reach them. Someone should have explained to him that he should expect a lot from his students' effort and intelligence but that he should not assume a lot about their previous training and experience.

If your child is frustrated by unreasonable demands from a teacher like Mr. Drake, you won't have great success by going directly to him. Chances are, Mr. Drake is a poor listener with an exaggerated opinion of his own skills. Still, if Mr. Drake won't listen to you, he will certainly listen to his boss. You need to go directly to the headmaster, say positive things about Drake, and suggest that the headmaster could share some of his wisdom and experience with the nice young man.

Miss Fairchild Miss Fairchild comes from a nice family, known to the headmaster, and was a graduate of the school herself. She graduated from college without a usable skill, so the family called in some favors to get her a position at her alma mater—your child's private school. Her college major was political science, so she has no training in classroom management. Fortunately, these are private school kids, so they are never too wild and unruly. The problem occurs at the beginning of each class and when they shift from one subject to another; Miss Fairchild's control is too casual, so a lot of time is lost in transitions. Less time on task leads to less achievement and poorer work habits.

This is another case where it will not be fruitful for the parent to complain to the teacher. She has no idea what she's doing wrong, and she doesn't know how to fix it. She may not even be aware of the problem. With a teacher like Miss Fairchild, the parent must go straight to the headmaster. Miss Fairchild needs peer assistance from more experienced teachers at the school, or guidance from the experienced hand of the headmaster herself.

Miss Kelly Miss Kelly is a problem because she doesn't even know your child's name or needs. She is giving him a grade, and that affects his self-image and his attitude, but she doesn't know him. She is usually a teacher of a noncore subject like art, music, or PE, and she may teach all of the children at the school. It will take her a long time to learn all the names; then after she does, she will be replaced by a new low-priced teacher and the cycle starts again.

The best way to deal with Miss Kelly is to meet her early in the year. Distinguish yourself from the crowd by making yourself available to help in the classroom or providing a gift or service for her department. Ask some specific questions about your child, and then say, "But of course, you can't answer that yet, because you don't know Johnny well. Keep it in mind, and I'll ask you again next month." You might even schedule a meeting well in advance, and send a question or two in writing, several weeks before the meeting. The idea is to make the teacher observe your child as an individual, not just another blurry face in the crowd.

Mr. Andrews Mr. Andrews was never a great teacher, but he was good enough when he was younger. Now that he has thirty years' experience under his belt, he no longer has the patience to tolerate normal childish behavior. His students no longer have the sense that he *likes* them, and school is not an exciting or pleasant place for them. The school doesn't really want to keep him on the faculty, but there are compelling reasons why they keep renewing his annual contract:

• They are afraid of expensive litigation. It is true that Mr. Andrews has no tenure protection, but there is precedent for the courts to rule that twenty years of employment leads to a reasonable expectation of continuing employment. There is the very real danger of losing an age discrimination case. And firing someone for cause may be tougher in a private school, because the school's quality of documentation against Mr. Andrews may not be strong. Private schools don't create and preserve written records the way public schools do.

- Many private school headmasters lack the nerve to get rid of the deadwood on the faculty. Over the years, the faculty effectively becomes self-selecting; only the teachers themselves decide when to leave the school.

- Mr. Andrews has made a lot of friends over the years, and some of them happen to sit on the school's board of trustees. He also has friends among the faculty and staff. These friends are not blind or stupid, and they wouldn't be unhappy if Mr. Andrews decided to take the leap, but they won't take part in pushing him off the faculty. So the school retains him to avoid creating a public uproar and a split in the social fabric of the school. And they do nothing, while they think about ways of sweetening the retirement pot.

Many parents, exasperated by the insoluble problems of the public schools, are very tempted by their perception of the private school experience: fewer bad teachers, a well-screened student body, better behavior. They recognize that the private school may have fewer resources, but that's a compromise they are willing to make . . . until their particular child is directly affected by an ineffective teacher and the absence of one of those resources. A common scenario that brings together bad teaching and unavailable resources, to the detriment of the child, is the lack of special educational testing and help in the private school.

Special Ed—Special Concerns

The public schools, by law, bear the responsibility to educate children with special educational needs. But private schools have no such obligation. They may voluntarily take on the task, and in fact there are private schools that specialize in special ed. But most private schools (especially the selective, competitive ones) don't want special ed pupils, don't want them slowing down their "brighter" pupils, and don't want to acquire a reputation as a place that welcomes special ed children.

So what happens if you have a child, already in a private school, who exhibits some need of special education? You soon learn that the private school wants to bury its head in the sand. What do you do?

Turn to the public schools for testing and help. They have the legal responsibility to help you, even if your child is not enrolled in the public school system. Depending on their backlog of other needy kids and the caseloads their psychologists are carrying, they will help you, willingly or unwillingly. In fact, if you request testing (and can document the need), they *must* do it, and must schedule it within a specified length of time (fifty days). They will do it at their location and on a schedule convenient to them, but they must do it.

While you can expect a report from the evaluation team that is as complete as possible, it is important to note that the testing and information gathering may be less thorough in the case of a private school client—not from lack of effort but simply because all the information about your child isn't already under the public school roof. Let's say your little boy has been tested and a disorder was recognized in speech and language. Based on the testing, an Individual Educational Plan (IEP) would be developed. Then you would go back to the private school, IEP in hand, and discuss what they are willing to do to implement it. They have no legal obligation to provide services beyond your enrollment contract, but they may be willing to help. If the IEP (or similar plan) requires minimal teacher time and preparation, and if the program does not disrupt other children or draw resources away from other children, the school may be willing to accommodate you. Even if they agree to do anything, they may insist that you, the parents, bear any incremental costs of the individualized program.

Whatever your child's special needs, bear in mind that the public school's obligation to help does not end with the testing; they are also obligated to help provide service. It is possible for your child to continue at the private school and also receive specialized speech, language, or other training from the local public school. This service is subject to some constraints: It must be provided during regular public school hours, and the parents must transport the child to the public school. So this plan might work for a once-a-week session, for example with a speech therapist, but would be impractical as a daily program.

If the private school is uncooperative and suggests that you find another school for your child, then you would be well advised to do it. You can't make them love your child if they don't; and you can't force them to bend to help him if they prefer not to. Private schools have always had intentions that exceeded their abilities, overestimating their ability to help children. So when they don't even have the intention to help your child, you *know* they don't have the ability. Public schools try to do everything, and consequently do many things badly. Private schools recognize that they live in a world of limited resources, and try to focus only on the things they can do well—and that doesn't include helping children with special ed needs.

The person at the private school who makes the decisions about those limited resources is the headmaster. He decides whether to stretch the school's focus to include children with special needs and requirements. There are various factors influencing his decisions.

THE HEADMASTER

Mr. Tweed enjoys his position as headmaster of Woodland Country Day School. After graduation from Princeton, he was too baby-faced to catch on with a big corporation, so he thought he would teach school for a few years. He taught eighth-grade history at Stanford Prep, and found that he liked teaching and liked the children. He became a popular and very effective teacher at Stanford Prep.

Through the students, he acquired a great deal of knowledge about the strengths and weaknesses of the elementary schools that feed students into Stanford Prep, including Woodland. When Woodland's headmaster retired, Mr. Tweed was interviewed and showed his understanding of the school, its problems, and its potential. Parents of current and past Woodland students spoke highly of him, and he was offered the job, even though he had no direct experience with elementary school. But his background seemed to offer the promise of shoehorning more Woodland students into the exclusive Stanford Prep, and as Woodland's board and parents know, that's what the game is all about.

Woodland is not the oldest, most established private school in town; it is still trying to make its reputation, and it will. The governing powers at Woodland are very conscious that education is a service industry. Just like the owners of a successful business, Woodland administrators have tried to find out precisely what the customer wants educationally, and Woodland tries very hard to provide exactly that.

Mr. Tweed's job title is headmaster, which means that he is the head "master," or head teacher, responsible for the educational direction of the school. But his job entails a lot more than that. The headmaster's main responsibility is fund-raising. The typical private school sets its tuition high enough to pay for operating costs (salaries, supplies, and property maintenance). But tuition is never high enough to cover capital expenses (the mortgage on the land and buildings, savings for emergencies or future building needs). Capital expenses must be made from gifts and bequests.

A boarding school gets most of its gifts from alumni. A private secondary school gets its gifts from alumni and current parents. A private elementary school gets almost nothing from alumni; it depends on current parents and grandparents for its gifts.

Money Matters at the Private School Money is tight in a private school. Banks don't like to loan money to schools, even for buildings. They determine loan eligibility by looking at the school's regular income stream, which doesn't include gifts. Without including gifts, the school's balance sheet looks very negative, so the school looks like a very poor risk. New buildings, for example, have to be paid for "out of pocket," from money already saved.

The tightness of money has an impact on other aspects of school operation as well.

• The headmaster must be very aware of "opportunity cost": Money spent on one thing becomes unavailable for other things. Private schools tend to spend their money much more efficiently.

• The Parents Association fund-raisers (usually for classroom materials) become significant. The headmaster has to thank and encourage the parent group, without letting them use their financial clout to take over control of the school.

• There is little in reserve for unexpected expenses. Very few private schools have any endowment at all.

• The headmaster has to emphasize nonfinancial rewards in keeping the faculty happy. She can't give teachers more money, so she has to deliver smaller classes, minimal behavior problems, and the freedom to be fairly autonomous within their own classrooms (autonomy works well as long as she hires good teachers, but . . .).

A major part of the headmaster's job is to be the lubrication between the three separate cogs that power the school: the faculty, the parents, and the board. He has to keep all three spinning together, not grinding against each other. Consequently, when a parent comes forth with a complaint about a teacher or about the school, that is exactly what the headmaster thinks about: the three power centers that drive the school.

The parents may get involved in the issue. Private school parents talk to each other constantly. In the circles that they travel, they often have other points of overlap besides the school. Opinions are shared, along with rumors of opinions, and opinions of opinions. The headmaster has to deal with problems quickly, before there is time for the ripples of opinion to ebb and flow out into the general community, possibly damaging the reputation of the school.

She would like the parents to bring problems directly to her, rather than complain to each other. But she really has no control over the parents. If there is a family that constantly spreads dissatisfaction, the headmaster could advise them that, if they aren't happy, they should leave the school. But the headmaster is not going to threaten expulsion of a family that has presented a problem *to her;* that would alienate the parents and would be more likely to start a stampede than to stop one. So you can go to the headmaster and complain directly about the bad teacher. This is unlike the situation in a public school, where you have to pretend that the problem is a mismatch between the child and the teacher.

As the parent of a private school child complaining about a teacher, you are in a much stronger position than a public school parent. And it is not because money talks; your tuition payments don't entitle you to run the school. Your big advantage is the absence of tenure in the private school. The headmaster always retains the option not to renew a contract for the next year; in unusual circumstances, she can terminate a contract in the middle of the year. And unions are rare among private schools.

Your complaints to the headmaster will be more effective if you maintain your loyalty, or at least the appearance of loyalty, to the school. You should always appear positive, always ask, "How can we make this wonderful school better?" Express concern that rumors of a bad teacher might affect the school's reputation in the community. Word of mouth is the only effective advertising for a school, and bad word of mouth can be very destructive.

Document, organize, and find allies, but don't flaunt the strength of your movement, and don't provoke a confrontation that may stiffen your opposition's resolve. In a small school, word gets out and secrets are few. It is more effective to have parallel complaints from a variety of sources, rather than a unified complaint from a single bloc of parents. Whisper, don't shout.

Ask around very discreetly, and you may find an ally in the faculty. Private schools do not have teacher unions that defend the indefensible, and other teachers may be happy to see the back of a bad teacher. But if the faculty decides to support a well-liked and well-respected colleague who is making life difficult for your child, Mr. Tweed may not be able to do anything in your behalf. The faculty is likely to have cultivated many friends among the board and parent organizations, and Mr. Tweed isn't about to lose a political fight on behalf of a single disgruntled family.

Perhaps you can find an ally among the school's board of trustees; after all, most of them are parents like you. Your friend on the board would not deal with your complaint officially, because it's not part of the board's responsibility. A headmaster's contract gives him the power to operate the school on a daily basis. The board makes policy and makes long-term decisions, but it does not interfere in the day-to-day running of the school. The board delegates all employment decisions to the headmaster, and promises not to get involved in hiring and firing. On the other hand, the headmaster would be a fool if he did not listen to the off-the-record opinions of board members.

In a private school, it *is* possible to get a bad teacher fired. Private school parents should keep in mind the ancient curse: "May you live to see your heart's desire!" If you go in howling for the teacher's head on a platter, you may get it. Then your child may suffer through the rest of the year with a succession of bad teachers instead of only one. Remember that private schools don't pay very well, and may not be able to hire top quality on short notice. All the good ones have already taken contracts elsewhere, and hot new prospects don't appear suddenly in the middle of the school year.

It's also a good idea to plan ahead, particularly in schools that have only one class per grade level. If you know that your child will be in Mrs. Duplin's class next year, and you think she is a bad teacher, do something now. Gather any pertinent information, document it, and deliver it to the headmaster before March, because that is the time when contracts are offered for the next year. If you get the facts to her in time, she will not need an excuse to withhold a contract from Mrs. Duplin. But if you wait to voice your opinion until after she has offered the contract and the teacher has signed it, you will need a much stronger case to get the headmaster to renege on the contract.

There is a lot more to private schools than just sending them a check and expecting all your educational problems to be solved. There are excellent reasons to choose a private school, if the tuition cost is not a burden to your budget. After all, what could you spend money on that would be more important than your child's future? But to spend the money and not get the results is throwing the money away, and your child with it. Don't expect a school to be your educational nirvana, just because they get their income from your pocket rather than the government's.

11

The Religious School and the Bad Teacher

Matthew was a fifth-grader at St. Vincent's parochial school. Entering the fifth grade marked a momentous change in Matthew's educational life, not just because the curriculum had become more challenging, but also because he moved from a self-contained classroom (with one teacher for all core subjects) to a departmentalized plan (with different teachers for different subjects).

Fifth grade also marked Matthew's first experience with Mrs. Holt, the notoriously difficult science teacher who had been the bane of St. Vincent's older students for many years. Sure enough, three months into the year, Matthew's parents were notified that their son was failing science. Although Matthew's mother had heard many of the stories about Mrs. Holt and her tyrannical attitude, she made an appointment with the teacher to discuss Matthew's difficulty. Repeatedly, the mother asked Mrs. Holt if something could be done to help Matthew succeed in science; repeatedly the teacher sidestepped the question. Finally the frustrated mother blurted, "Look, I don't want to seem insistent, but Matt has never done failing work in science before. There must be *something* I can do—with your help—to get him on the right track."

The teacher just shrugged her shoulders. "The bottom line is this, Mrs. Smith. If Matthew doesn't have it up *here*"—the teacher pointed to her temple—"then there's nothing anyone can do to *put* it up here."

Was Mrs. Holt ever reprimanded for making the outrageous comment? Did she ever offer the evidence that led to her hasty and damning conclusion? Has she ever asked herself why she bothers to teach at all, if a child's learning is entirely predetermined by his IQ? Certainly not. She has never been challenged for giving up on children so easily; and she has continued to torture children at that very real school.

That's because religious schools make their own rules. Like independent schools, they are not bound by the extensive regulations of the Education Code that govern every aspect of public school life. They can hire and fire whom they like, and they can supervise teachers as loosely or as closely as they wish. Since religious schools pay so little, they try to give teachers more freedom in lieu of more money. So the poorly paid religious school teacher is less constrained by rules and less controlled by supervision. Therefore, it is not surprising that religious schools employ more than their share of bad teachers.

Religious Schools and the Quality Paradox

Just as there are churches and synagogues of every shade along the theological spectrum, there are many dif-

ferent kinds of religious schools. Any attempt to catego-
rize church- or synagogue-run schools must therefore be
imperfect, but some simplification is necessary. This
chapter will divide religious schools into two distinct
types, the "dogma delivery system" and the "family magnet"; naturally, there will be schools that fall somewhere
in the middle.

The classic religious school is a dogma delivery system. The congregation has plenty of members, enough to
supply children to fill a school. The congregation members feel very strongly about their religion. One of their
biggest objections to the local public school is that it is
godless; there is no religion in the classroom, and the
moral lessons taught there are either insufficient or inconsistent with their religious teachings. Since it is important to them that their children learn in an
environment that reinforces their religious beliefs, they
operate a school on the church or synagogue property,
using the already existing classrooms. There are minimal
capital costs. The teachers are hired more for their religious orientation than for their teaching skill or experience, so they don't cost much either. The tuition is kept
very low so all the congregation members can afford to
send their children.

The classes in these schools tend to be large but very
well behaved. In many churches that tend toward funda-
mentalism, behavior is seen as a personal battle between
God and Satan; any lack of docility is the work of the
devil and is not tolerated. The school administration
tends to be authoritarian and the discipline may be punitive or even physical. Parents are not encouraged to question the philosophy or operation of the school. The school
is subsidized by the religious institution, and the parents'

financial contribution is not sufficient to give them any clout.

Admission to the school is either limited to members of the congregation, or priority is given to them. This is usually not a problem, as nonmembers might not feel comfortable in that community anyway. These are parochial schools, in both meanings of the word: "parochial" means "pertaining to a parish"; it also means "narrow in viewpoint or outlook."

The dogma delivery system model is typical of the Catholic school systems and the fundamentalist Christian schools. It also includes Orthodox Jewish yeshivas and church schools operated by ethnic religious groups (like Armenian Orthodox) who are trying to preserve their culture and language, as well as their religion.

At the other end of the scale, very close in philosophy to the independent schools, are the family magnet church schools. They are sponsored by smaller church parishes that want to attract new families, or by a church organization other than a parish church. They tend to be less doctrinaire and less evangelistic; that is, they aren't trying to convert anyone to their religion or impress specific religious beliefs on their students. Admission to the school is not restricted, although preference may still be given to member families.

Families who send their children to family magnet schools like the idea of religion in the classroom, but they want a nondenominational presence that is more ethical than doctrinaire. They want children to think about morals and religion, but not memorize doctrines or take things on blind faith. Parents' main objection to the local public school is its lack of quality, not its lack of godliness. They are looking for quality education and they are willing to pay more than the typical parochial school tuition.

Family magnet schools, recognizing their clients' desires, try harder to provide quality education. They hire teachers for their skills rather than their doctrinal purity. They also tend to listen more to parents and are usually more sympathetic and accommodating when problems occur. Discipline is not seen as a battle against the forces of darkness, and therefore tends to be less punitive.

These schools are more likely to be creations of the Episcopal, Quaker, and Congregational churches, or of the Catholic Church's Society of Jesus (the Loyola schools and colleges).

What happens when a church or synagogue establishes a school in order to attract members to the community, and the plan succeeds? Let's say the school becomes well known for its quality education, and families join the congregation in order to get their children into the school. At this point, the admissions department comes under pressure from all sides. The church or synagogue begins to insist that the congregation families' children be accepted in preference to much more capable noncongregation children. At one local school, the admissions process predetermines three kindergarten reading groups: The upper group is made up of unaffiliated children who scored high in ability, the middle group is made up of siblings of older children in the school, and the remedial group is made up of church or synagogue members. As the school attracts more families to the church, the quality of the students declines, and the quality of the school declines with it.

If the school tries to maintain its quality by maintaining its independence, sooner or later the church or synagogue will assert its ownership position. Often this happens when the congregation gets a new, more doctrinaire priest or rabbi. The school is then faced with a decision; it must yield to the church or synagogue and become more of a dogma delivery system, or it must break loose and become an independent school. Most of the great private schools (and some colleges) of this country began as religious schools and later became independent. But breaking loose is a very expensive and energy-consuming process, so it rarely happens. Most religious schools just buckle under, abandon the quest for quality, and become dogma delivery systems. In time, the good teachers leave those schools, and the bad teachers begin to accumulate.

Typical Bad Teachers in Religious Schools

Religious schools pay very poorly—even less than independent private schools. Once upon a time this was not a problem, because they could staff their schools with nuns, or with young women too nice to face the business world. But the world has changed. There are fewer women working for nothing. Today, anyone with even minimal skills can find alternatives that pay much better than teaching in a religious school. So the religious schools have to find teachers who are strongly motivated by nonfinancial rewards, or settle for the less capable teachers. As you might imagine, religious schools accumulate more than their share of bad teachers.

Some of the bad teachers you have already met can be found in religious schools. The uncertified teacher who can't diagnose learning problems is a fixture at religious schools. So is "the labeler," who accepts the permanent file as truly permanent, and never gives a kid a chance for a fresh start. You will also find "the stickler," who attaches great importance to unimportant subjects (penmanship, spelling) and doesn't focus on critical areas like reading and arithmetic.

Nearly every religious school employs at least one "antique," the teacher who hasn't had a new idea in her head for thirty years. "The old ideas are the best," this teacher insists. Some old ideas are the best, because they have stood the test of time; but some other ideas don't become best just because they are old. The "antique" never stops to figure out which is which.

Religious schools are also havens for teachers like Mr. Hughes, for whom there are no shades of gray. He is convinced that the difference between good and evil is as clearly defined as the difference between night and day, and he is sure that his concept of *right* is the only possible version. There is a little bit of Mr. Hughes in many religious school teachers and in the religious school curriculum. And it should be there; one of the things that attracts parents to church schools is the schools' rejection of moral relativism and situational ethics. Children need to learn what is right and what is wrong . . . as long as they aren't learning it from fanatics.

In addition to the bad teachers who are common to all types of schools, the religious schools have a few who are unique, or whom we find at religious schools in unusually toxic forms. Here are a few examples:

Ms. Lowell is found only in a religious school. Her life is infused with the power of her faith. If she is teaching music, the songs are all hymns or have some religious connotation. If she is teaching in the classroom, the history is all Bible oriented and the science creationist. The

English essays have themes like "Imagine you are a shep-
herd in the Holy Land" or "How I resist temptation."
Even the math problems are questions like "How many
more pilgrims visited the shrine on Tuesday than on
Thursday?"

Ms. Lowell may not be a bad teacher for your child.
She may have a great deal of enthusiasm, and she may
communicate that enthusiasm to your child. You would
love to see your child enthusiastic about being strong in
character, mind, and body; you would love to see your
child enthusiastic about learning, whatever the subject
matter, because it opens up the mind. But if the enthusiasm isn't there, then the mind isn't being opened, and all
your child gets from Ms. Lowell is a very narrow view of
the world.

Mr. Niano had been a teacher in another part of the
world. He came to America with his family as part of a
program sponsored by the church. The church found employment for his wife at a local factory; her skills would
qualify her for a much better job, but she speaks no English. Mr. Niano knows only a few words of English, so
he could not find a teaching job in public or private
schools. The church essentially created a job for him in
its own school, although neither the school nor the
church has members who speak Mr. Niano's language.
The children were taught: "Never make fun of someone
who speaks with an accent. The accent only means that
he speaks more languages than you do." This would be
good advice if Mr. Niano actually spoke more languages
than his native language, but his English is so poor the
children can't understand him.

Under pressure from the parents, the church school
acknowledged the problem of having a teacher who

didn't understand English. So they assigned Mr. Niano to team teach with another teacher. The other teacher handles English and reading. Mr. Niano now teaches math to *two* classes who can't understand him, and teaches a history that is foreign to him in a language he doesn't speak. Parents and children are told that "charity begins at home," and are encouraged to be pleased about their part in helping the Niano family adjust to life in America. It's easy for the church to say; they aren't the ones making the sacrifice.

Mrs. Whittler has been a member of the parish for umpteen years, and her husband has served on parish committees and boards forever. Their friends are the old guard power structure of the parish, and Mrs. Whittler is the source of most of their information about the school. Mrs. Whittler is a sacred cow; neither the minister nor the school head would dare to fire her from the faculty, afraid that the old guard will rise up and howl.

Mrs. Whittler and her generation are preparing to retire. It's time to hand over the reins to the next generation, but they don't want to do it. Mrs. Whittler doesn't like the way the next generation is raising children. Those children have no respect for their elders, they don't know how to behave, they lack self-control, and so on. Mrs. Whittler's solution to the decay of modern youth is to humiliate any child who fails to meet her standards. She announces failing grades to the entire class, she calls children names like "dunce" or "emptyhead," and she makes all punishments into public spectacles. The cardinal sin is showing lack of respect for one's elders; a child with an unbroken spirit is a personal affront to Mrs. Whittler. She says that "pride goeth before a fall," but she makes sure that each child falls before her, pride or no pride.

Ms. Pointer teaches in the middle grades at the local parochial school. Her hero is Bishop Diego de Landa, the patron saint of Catholic education. In 1562 in Mexico City, Bishop de Landa ordered the destruction of every book ever written in the Mayan language (only three books escaped and still exist). In one stroke, Bishop de Landa wiped out an entire culture: the collected thoughts, dreams, history, and ideas of a once great civilization.

Bishop de Landa has been an inspiration to dogmatic Catholic educators everywhere. They have continued his crusade in schools, to crush independent thought and to suppress unconquered minds. At Ms. Pointer's school, as at other parochial schools, the curriculum is strong on rote memorization, weak on logic; strong on math computation, weak on math concepts; strong on penmanship, weak on creative composition.

Like Mr. Hughes's students, Ms. Pointer's students sit up straight, march in perfect lines, and then explode when they get out from under her heavy thumb. In school, the lockers and the notebooks must always be orderly. A homework assignment for Ms. Pointer must meet exacting specifications, including a proper heading, the approved numbering system, precisely formatted paragraphs, and a distinct lack of erasures. Every draft must be a final draft, because errors in style detract more than errors of substance.

Sister Mary, the school principal, has a very high opinion of Ms. Pointer. After all, her children are always well behaved, and the work displayed on the bulletin boards is exemplary. Sister Mary knows that Ms. Pointer has a reputation as "demanding," but she approves of the way Ms. Pointer is upholding the standards of the school. Sister Mary isn't at the children's homes, so she can't tally up the cost of Ms. Pointer's obsessiveness. And Sister Mary closes her ears to reports that Ms. Pointer enforces her iron discipline with the flat side of a ruler.

Beat the Devil: Discipline in the Parochial School

Many parents choose parochial schools for their children because they are appalled by what they hear about the public schools. They fear for the safety of children who must go into the drug-infested armed camp of the big-city public school—or at least, that's the way they perceive it. They see the parochial school as a haven of safety in a dangerous world, and they want that kind of safety for their own precious children.

Of course, when the trains run on time, you don't really want to look too closely at what measures have been taken to make those trains timely. Uniformed kids walking in orderly lines is an attractive image, if you don't look between the lines. But how did the school achieve this cultivated image of grace and precision? Does their unison reflect remarkable self-discipline, or were the children browbeaten into submission? Or worse?

Corporal punishment has almost disappeared from schools in the civilized world. Among the Western nations, only the English-speaking countries ever allowed corporal punishment. Of the English-speaking countries, only the United States still permits it. In the public schools of the United States, it is rare outside the Southern states. The few places that still permit paddling, caning, or other forms of corporal punishment are mostly

Southern rural schools and church schools run by fundamentalist, evangelical, and/or Baptist churches.

"Church groups that claim literal belief in the Bible valued the use of hitting as a disciplinary tool," according to a study at the University of Kentucky. They tend to interpret children's misbehavior as the devil's work, and they believe that "corporal punishment instills character, obedience, and humility—traits needed to ward off the devil." To justify their actions, they quote passages from the Old Testament. Nowhere in the New Testament does Jesus suggest the use of violence against children.

Most schools disapprove of corporal punishment on philosophical grounds; it is simply unspeakable for an adult to hit helpless little children. Even the schools that have no philosophical compunction about it have discovered that corporal punishment simply doesn't work. It may mark a pause in a pattern of misbehavior, but it won't stop the misbehavior. It's more likely to increase the misbehavior and drive it underground, creating a long-term adversarial relationship between teachers and students.

Discipline is not synonymous with punishment; punishment is merely the least effective form of discipline. In a good school, discipline is achieved by the use of alternatives to corporal punishment: time-outs, student-teacher conferences and contracts, peer crisis intervention and counseling, positive reinforcement, behavior modification, and group discussions. In a great school, discipline becomes internal self-discipline. But even in a great school, normal children will sometimes be rowdy, and children will still misbehave or "act out" as a way to get attention. But they will get the attention they crave without incurring the wrath of God or provoking the heavy hand of a child abuser.

Ideally, a school's discipline policy should be made known to a parent before the child ever enters the school, particularly if the discipline includes corporal punishment. When a parent signs the enrollment contract, he is accepting the school's policies, including their discipline policy; it comes with the territory. The parent should be aware of the policy and either accede to it or choose not to enroll the child. It isn't sufficient to assume that the policy is good because it keeps everyone else's kids under control; there is no guarantee that it will never be applied to your own child. It is important to note that the courts have recognized that a school policy endorsing corporal punishment does not grant that school free license to indulge in child abuse; there are limits to the extent of permissible corporal punishment, even in church schools. Abusing children is not a protected exercise of religious freedom.

What do you do if your child has been subjected to an abusive teacher? Or, more generally, what do you do if your child encounters any kind of a bad teacher in a church school?

Pointing the Finger in the Religious School

When your child is enrolled in a religious school and has a bad teacher, you have a big problem. There are lots of factors working against you, and there is a strong possibility that you may end up with no satisfactory solution. This is especially true at church schools of the dogma delivery system type.

From the religious school's point of view, your child is getting a private school education at a very low price, subsidized by the congregation. In exchange for this "bargain," many religious school administrators expect you to be very grateful for whatever you get and to keep quiet when you are not getting what you think you deserve. Complaining is considered very bad form, akin to looking a gift horse in the mouth.

The religious school's priorities don't list your child anywhere. They don't have a legal responsibility to educate him, as the public schools do. Nor have they taken enough money from you to feel any obligation to keep you happy, as the independent schools do. You've got no stick and you've got no carrot.

In fact, church schools of the fundamentalist type don't answer to parents at all; they answer to their own church leaders, most of whom are celibate or beyond childbearing age. The way they see it, the school's job is to deliver their version of religious truth to the youth of the parish. They want to preach to the young converted, and if you are a complainer or an independent thinker who seems to be straying from the flock, they will happily replace you with another, more compliant follower.

There are other problems as well. Religious schools tend to be small. There may be only one self-contained class per grade, making it impossible to transfer within the school. In a departmentalized structure, there may be only one history teacher, only one math teacher, and so on. Not only can your child not escape the bad teacher, he will have to face that same teacher for years. There may be no escape.

Nor can you hold religious school teachers to the same standards you expect from public school teachers. You can't object that your child's teacher is too much the zealot. When the school's stated goal is indoctrination rather than education, that doesn't leave you much room to complain about an excess of indoctrination or a short-fall of education.

In truth, most religious schools won't let you object to much of anything. They take their curriculum, their discipline code, their faculty, and all their policies, and wrap them up in a religious robe. Since the school is an extension of the church or synagogue, the curriculum is construed as an extension of God's hand on earth. Criticism of any aspect of the school becomes an attack on the commonly held religious beliefs of the congregation. I know more than one set of parents who were compelled to change schools *and churches* after a disagreement with church school officials.

Moreover, the "robe" that religious school officials wrap themselves in may be tangible as well as abstract. In many religious schools, the nominal head of the school is a clergyman or member of a religious order. The actual administrative duties may be delegated to a lesser official, but even that person is likely to be a nun, or a deacon, or a lay preacher. It is hard for a parent to separate the educational from the religious when complaining to a nun—or about a nun.

So is there anything you can do about a bad teacher in a religious school? It depends on what type of religious school it is. If it is the dogma delivery system of a flourishing parish, there is very little you can do. The school doesn't have to give you an inch. Its policies and procedures are sanctioned by the church or synagogue, and you are unlikely to convince them that God is on the side of change. Nor can you realistically threaten to remove your child if accommodations aren't made, because they would be very happy to see you go.

If you push too hard, they will push back—maybe on your child. They will make the child feel isolated, and they will unite faculty and administration in nudging your child out of the school. How do you fight back? You don't. You ask yourself, "Why did I ever want my child in this bizarre school in the first place?" And then you move him, and later wish you had moved him sooner. If the religious school doesn't want him, don't hang on by your fingernails, because that school is not the best place for him.

If your child is happy there, and his friends are there, and your friends are there, and you still feel comfortable in that congregation, you have many good reasons to allow your child to stay. But you must try to do something about the bad teaching. What can you do?

First, you recognize that the school has no obligation to you, that its obligation is to the congregation.

So you go and speak to the priest or rabbi, telling him or her what a good member you have been for so many years. You tell him or her how happy you are at the school, and how active and supportive you have been. Then you mention that your child has a problem at the school that is damaging his education. And you point out that, more important, *because* religion and education are so inextricably entwined at the school, the problem in the education area is spilling over and damaging his faith in his religion.

Remember that in the religious school, particularly the small church school, there is strength in numbers. If the problem is a bad teacher, you can be sure that there is an impact on other children. Encourage parents of other affected children to go the priest or rabbi and speak their minds, too. Don't, however, suggest that they descend on the administration in a group. The administration will resist what it perceives to be an organized effort and you will be labeled a troublemaker. The other parents should go individually. They can admit that they have talked informally with other parents, but if they focus on their own individual children, it will not give the impression of an organized movement. The priest or rabbi can think of himself (or herself) as dynamic if he or she acts to head off a groundswell of complaint; he or she can't think of himself as dynamic in giving in to a disgruntled group.

What will you get for your efforts? Perhaps no direct action by the congregation, because the congregation wants to allow the school principal the illusion of autonomy; but you will get a meeting with the school principal, and the priest or rabbi will have instructed the principal to be responsive—or at least to be a good listener. Once you have the principal's attention, you can change your tactics. You are no longer playing the religion card; you are appealing to the professionalism of the principal. The school itself has no obligation to you, but the principal must have some personal pride, some desire to give the best education possible. Play on that, and see if two adults, reasoning together, can make life better for your child.

Keep in mind that the principal may have very little that she *can* offer you. She can't fire the teacher and find another one, she can't transfer your child to another class if there isn't one, and she doesn't have aides and other resources to shift into your child's classroom to compensate for bad teaching. Her staff has neither the training nor the materials to deal with any child's specific learning

difficulties. You need to think about what you will ask
for before you meet with the principal. And if her suggestions for remediation seem too weak, too ill defined, or
simply too late to help your child, you must consider
transferring your child to another, more responsive
school.

On the other hand, if the school is a family magnet type
for a smaller or newer congregation, there is hope of
doing something about a bad teacher. This type of school
is not the captive in-house mouthpiece for the church or
synagogue; to be successful, this school has to appeal to
families outside the congregation. Because of that, its religious message must be muted and diluted. The school
can't pretend that its curriculum, policies, and staff are
exempt from criticism because they are extensions of
God's right hand. Just to exist, these schools have to offer
quality education to satisfied families; and that means
that they have to listen and respond to parents.

This type of religious school is similar to the independent private school in many ways. In both schools, the
families are strongly ethical and moderately religious;
church memberships are largely mainstream Protestant,
Jewish, and Catholic. In short, they are parents who
want learning to proceed in a safe environment where
values are important, character is emphasized, and effort
is rewarded.

When you go to the school principal, speak well of the
school and all the benefits your child has derived from it.
Then describe your child's problem as calmly and posi-
tively as possible. The family magnet school principal
will probably lend a receptive ear. But you can't get blood

from a stone; the principal can't give you what he doesn't
have. Be prepared before your meeting. Know what you
will be asking for, and make sure it is a reasonable request that the principal is capable of providing, something that will not strain the resources of the school, or
require the principal to ask too much of any teachers.

The Bottom Line

Think about what you want your child to become by
the end of sixth grade or twelfth grade. Very few parents
would list attributes like "knows the periodic table, has
mastered precalculus, can list the amendments in the Bill
of Rights." Memorization of content does not define a
well-rounded or well-educated person.

A parent wants her child to love learning, to strive for
excellence, to treat others with respect, and to behave
with upright character. These are the virtues that will
carry the child to success and happiness in life. And these
are the virtues that a good church school should impart.
The church school your child attends may have a number
of bad teachers and the content of its curriculum may not
be all that you had hoped. But in the end, it comes down
to this: Is the school turning out the kind of graduates
that *you want your own child to be?*

The answer may well be yes. And for your child to
reach graduation day at that school, he may have to endure some bad teachers whom he cannot escape. You and
your child will have to weigh the benefits of a religious
school education, and decide just how much bad teaching
you are willing to endure. The bargain works like this: A
religious school education has the best qualities of a pri-

vate school education, at half the price or even less. In exchange, you have to accept the religious school as it is; acknowledge that you have minimal ability to make them change anything that is deficient.

If you or your child are so unhappy that you must leave the school, then you must consider the alternatives, none of which is an ideal school free of bad teachers. You may decide to tolerate the problems at the school you know, rather than transferring to another school whose problems may be worse.

12

Education Begins at Home

Jimmy graduated from elementary school in June, although even he has a hard time remembering just which school he graduated from. You see, Jimmy attended four different schools in the last six years. His parents moved him from school to school, hoping to find one that could ignite a spark of enthusiasm, something to light the lamp of knowledge. Now, as they look back over the four schools Jimmy attended, they wonder why they made some of the transfers. Jimmy's experiences have taught them that no school is perfect; and they have learned that in their quest for perfection, they made some hasty choices. Now they regret their heat-of-the-moment decisions and wonder if the flaw is "not in our schools but in ourselves," to paraphrase Shakespeare. If they had it to do all over again, they would have been more tolerant of minor flaws in the schools, in the teachers, and perhaps even in Jimmy.

Jimmy's parents are concerned too late, because their good intentions have created some unintended negative consequences for Jimmy.

• Jimmy has developed the attitude that his difficulties are always somebody else's fault; that if he doesn't
succeed in school, it must be the school's fault and not
his own. The fact is, Jimmy has brought nothing to the
table, but he still expects to be fed. His parents have
helped him blame everyone else, so he has no need to take
the responsibility for his own actions.

• Jimmy has acquired the belief that when the going
gets tough, it's okay to quit. No one endorses suffering as
a character-building program, but in real life, bad things
do happen and people *do* learn from them. The phrase
"No pain, no gain" may be a cliche but it is not without a
kernel of truth. Children can't find out how much they
are capable of until they push their limits. Jimmy hasn't
pushed himself hard enough to learn how much he is capable of achieving.

• Jimmy has been the classmate of every twelve-
year-old in town. And he gets along perfectly well with
all of them, but he has no really close friends. Jimmy has
learned not to get too attached to any friend, because experience tells him that next year they'll be apart again.

• Jimmy didn't just switch schools, he also switched
curricula several times. There were some lessons he
learned repeatedly, and other lessons he missed entirely.
School hopping left some odd holes in his store of knowledge, odd weaknesses in his educational fundamentals
that are bound to show up unexpectedly in the future.

• Where did Jimmy end up in seventh grade? Unfortunately, not at the best school for him. Midway through
his sixth grade year, his parents applied to a selective private school, but Jimmy was rejected. His academic record
was, by then, quite undistinguished, so his parents were
anticipating a rejection. But his parents didn't know that

Jimmy's application was doomed as soon as the admissions office saw how often Jimmy had bounced from school to school. In the absence of another explanation, the admissions officers assumed that Jimmy was a problem (in which case the school didn't want Jimmy) or that the parents were chronically dissatisfied (in which case the school didn't want the parents).

The Bitter End

Davy's parents have another problem. Davy has not bounced around from school to school. In fact, his parents have been happy with Davy's school until recently. This year Davy has had a certifiably bad teacher, and the school is aware of the problem but hasn't done enough to solve the problem. Davy has muddled through heroically, but he is finally at about the end of his rope. Davy has reached the point that his health has been affected; it's a race between stress, depression, and ulcers to see which will finish him off. Davy's parents don't want to change schools, but they don't want to force their son to finish out the year with this rotten teacher. What can they do?

How much time is left in the year? If it's only six or eight weeks, and there is an adult at home, then they might consider just taking him out of school. If he is in a public school, he can always go back. In one sense, public school is like home—home is wherever, when you go there, they have to take you in. So he can always go back in the fall, and he will rejoin his regular classmates. There is zero chance that the school will hold him back and make him repeat a grade, even if he has missed two months of school. Besides, the parents will try to keep his work up to date while he's out. The school may consider Davy truant, so they may need a doctor to certify that Davy is sick, or that Davy would be sick if he had to face that teacher.

Another approach is for parents to use the opportunity to take an extended vacation and, of course, take Davy along. Or have Davy visit relatives out of town for a few weeks. The marginal value of a day at school is practically zero; the marginal value of a week is still barely measurable. Even if Davy misses several weeks of school, he hasn't missed much.

If he is in a private school, they can still take him out and have him return in the fall, if they make arrangements with the school before they act. The school will expect the parents to continue paying tuition in order to hold the space, and will expect Davy to keep his work up to date.

If Davy leaves school and spends six or eight weeks in the library, he will return far ahead of his classmates. A child learns more in an hour at the library than he does in a really good day at school. Keep this in mind if you are moderately satisfied with your child's teachers but unhappy with your child's school: Don't change schools, change libraries.

What can parents do if it is too early in the school year to just drop out? If it is still late autumn or winter, and Davy is in a public school with a certifiably bad teacher, and it's clear that the school and district won't do anything, how do you save Davy? You need to weigh all of the alternatives and compare them to the perils of leaving Davy in his current classroom.

Going Private

It's December. Having read Part One of this book, you are convinced that your child has a bad teacher. Using Part Two, you have tried to get help from the school and district, but no help is forthcoming. Although you know that expensive private schools have bad teachers, too, you feel that the teachers and administrators at your public school are either unwilling or unable to help your child. But before you move him or her from public school to private school, there are some things you should first consider.

If you are applying to a selective private school, you had better plan far in advance. They are at full enrollment, so they will rarely have space available during the year, unless another family moves away. A top school will have an admissions time line that goes something like this: Testing and interviews are conducted during December or January; your completed application will be due by February 1; you can expect notification of acceptance or rejection in mid-March; and school starts in September. As you will note, this schedule does not provide your child with immediate relief from a bad teacher.

Less selective private schools may have a "rolling admissions" policy, which means that they aren't tied to inflexible deadlines. You can apply at any time through the winter and late spring, perhaps even into the summer. These schools close admission for each grade whenever classroom capacity is reached, and the new students start in September.

The least selective private schools may have space available at midyear. This could solve your problem, but

it should also raise a few questions in your mind: Why
does the school have space? Is there something undesir-
able about the school? Whatever school you are considering, you need to know more about it before you entrust
your child to them. If you know any families currently at
the school, talk to them and ask if they are satisfied. Any
alternative can look-good to desperate parents. An honest
response from someone you trust can prevent you from
settling for the first available "port in a storm."

Stop by the school yard and check out the kids when
they are least supervised, at lunchtime or recess; see how
they treat each other and how they relate to the staff.
This will give you much more realistic insight into the
educational climate of the school than you would get
from visiting a classroom, which is a situation made artificial by your presence.

You must, of course, *ask* the school administrators
about their priorities, and listen politely to their answers.
But if you want to see proof of the school's philosophy,
check the class schedules. How much time is reserved for
reading and for other basic subjects? How much is devoted to the arts, music, or religion? If the school's priorities and yours don't match, pass on this opportunity.
Administrators can say almost anything to make you
happy, but schedules don't lie about the school's real priorities.

If you are still in doubt about the "rightness" of this
school for your child, look at the textbooks. Are they from
major mainstream publishers, or are they from niche
publishers that cater to certain narrow points of view?
Do they seem too easy for your child's grade level and
performance? Many texts have been "dumbed down"
two grade levels, which makes them inappropriate for

good private schools. Don't be surprised to find, then, that the best private schools compensate for simplistic texts by bumping the texts down a grade, using a sixth grade English textbook for fifth grade instruction, and so on. And don't be surprised to discover that some progressive private schools don't use textbooks for science and social studies at all. This can be a very good thing, if the school has developed alternative materials to excite and motivate its students. Just ask to see the nontext materials in action, and inquire as to why they were chosen.

Finally, ask the administrators what they feel is distinctive about their school. Ask them how much outside reading is required. And ask them what they do to engage bright, bored kids.

If the school's priorities match your philosophy, if it has space and accepts your child, then you need to smooth her transition from public to private school. It is not a good idea for her to leave one school on Friday and start cold at the new school on Monday. Schedule your child's first day at the new school for the beginning of the semester or other grading period, or perhaps immediately after a vacation. Before she starts, get the new textbooks so she can acclimatize herself to the new class. Jumping into a new school can be like jumping into a moving airplane. Find out exactly where the class is, and what they have covered in those textbooks, so your favorite student can get up to speed quickly. If there is anything your child has not been taught, I suggest you have her tutored. Better yet, if it is possible, try to hire her new teacher as the tutor; he knows exactly what to cover, and it gives teacher and student a chance to get to know each other. If the school has a policy, as some do, of not allowing teachers to accept money for tutoring their enrolled stu dents, ask if you can hire the school's teacher from the next lower grade. Or perhaps the new school can suggest a tutor who is familiar with the school's curriculum and expectations. The tutoring may not succeed in getting your child entirely caught up to the class by the time she starts at the new school, but it will keep her from feeling panicky and overwhelmed.

Going Public

There are many communities with excellent public school systems. In those communities, the private schools cannot compete with their publicly funded counterparts unless they are extraordinarily good, or unless they appeal to some special niche in the educational marketplace.

And there are many communities where the private and public schools are equal in quality. Wherever you live, there may be very good reasons to move a child from a private school to a public school. For one thing, private schools are expensive. Parents can do a lot for their children educationally if they aren't spending that money on tuition. They can hire tutors if the child needs them; they can buy professional equipment and coaching for anything the child is interested in; they can give the child an open account at the local bookstore; they can buy him state-of-the-art computers; they can send her on tours of the museums of Europe, and archaeological digs in the summer; they can send the family on Earthwatch expeditions; they can buy zero-coupon bonds for a college education. There are more fascinating ways to enrich a child's education other than paying tuition.

And private schools are not the right choice for everyone. Many children who are now in private schools would be better served by the public schools. For example:

- a child with special educational needs
- a child who is a poor psychological match for a private or religious school because he is too lively, too independent of thought, or not sufficiently pious
- a child who has the desire to excel but hasn't the intellectual tools to excel in a competitive private school
- a stressed-out child who is trying to meet expectations (either her own or her parents') that exceed her abilities
- a child with an interest in particular programs, like high-level competitive sports, that are better in the public schools
- a child with a major commitment to an out-of-school activity (such as sports, music, health maintenance, family care) that leaves little time for a heavy academic load
- a child who chooses the right friends anywhere; that child will end up with good values and a good education wherever she goes

Transferring to Another District

When your child is having problems with a bad teacher and the district is obstinate, parents should consider moving him to an entirely different school district. This may not always be the most convenient option, geographically or logistically, but it may get your child through the year, after which he can return to a different teacher at his local school.

If there is a district that is attractive to you, the first thing you need to find out is whether interdistrict transfers are permitted by the law in your state and by the districts involved. Some states, particularly those that can't get up the nerve to adopt vouchers but want to introduce the element of competition into their public school systems, encourage open transfers. The theory is that districts will have to improve, or lose their students to districts that try harder. In some other states, students can be effectively restricted to their district of residence.

The last thing you want to do is to ask your home district for a transfer out. They don't want to transfer any child out, because their state funding depends on enrollment. They will tell you it's impossible, or not allowed, or something that sounds like "It is forbidden," when it really means, "We don't want you to." Instead, begin by getting the approval of the district you wish to transfer *into.* They really want you and the funding you represent; let them handle the paperwork. And how do you choose the district to transfer into?

Geography Pick a district that is within twenty minutes of your home, or preferably closer. Since the school will not transport your child, you will have to deliver her to and from school each day. The issue is not just the time you will spend going to and from school. Remember that your child will form friendships with schoolmates, so you will be traveling to that other community for many social occasions, too.

Quality Once again, it's important to recall that the quality of a school is dependent on the quality of its students. You want your child to attend a school filled with bright, hardworking students who model excellent character and values. Look for a school district that prides itself on these qualities, perhaps one that surrounds a university—faculty children contribute to an excellent environment for learning.

Look in the newspaper files for standardized test scores for all the local schools and districts. Test scores are a good scorecard to measure school quality. Though they aren't a measure of all the important things that make up a child, and don't pretend to be, they are a good indicator of the few things that everyone agrees are important: reading, writing, and arithmetic.

Educators, particularly those in low-scoring districts, tend to minimize the importance of test scores, saying that children are too diverse and multifaceted to be reduced to a small set of numbers. They say this because, too often, their scores are low and they don't want to be held accountable. They also argue that it's not fair to compare rich kids with poor kids, and that's true. Some schools in poor neighborhoods should be heaped with prizes and awards when they get their average up to the thirtieth percentile, while other, wealthier schools are doing nothing to improve their already bright students. But from your point of view, it isn't important to you whether a school has reached the eightieth percentile by hard work or by accidents of fortunate birth. What you care about is that your child will be among high-achieving, successful children, and will absorb the positive values of that environment.

Home Schooling

Robert and his family live in a nice suburb with a good school system, but that didn't prevent Robert from getting a bad teacher. His parents did all the right things— they tried reasoning with the teacher, discussing the problem with the principal, and working with the school district, but they were stonewalled. It was clear that Robert would be stuck with that destructive teacher for the rest of a long year. Desperate, the family looked into the local private schools, but the good ones had no space and the weaker ones weren't worth the cost. Besides, Robert's father was concerned that his job might be downsized out of existence, so it was not a good time to commit to additional expenses. Robert's mother even considered taking a part-time job, in order to pay for Robert's private school tuition; but the only jobs available were minimum wage positions. Finally, the family decided that Robert's mother would teach Robert at home. They entered into home schooling with some trepidation. Their first concern was about Robert's mother *being* just another bad teacher for Robert, because she had no teaching credential. In fact, she didn't have any kind of college degree at all.

Moreover, Robert's family, having rejected the option of traditional schooling, felt isolated in their decision, until they tapped into the local home schooling network. Without carrying a banner or joining a crusade, they found that they were not alone at all but part of a vital million-child march of home schoolers. And they found that the parade included people with a wide variety of philosophies, but the majority were families just like themselves.

Some had chosen home schooling for religious reasons. They were unhappy with the banishment of God from the public schools, and they wanted to raise their children in a more religious, often fundamentalist, Christian atmosphere.

Some opted to educate their children at home for moral and ethical reasons. They were concerned that the schools were either teaching situational ethics or neglecting ethics entirely, so the schools were undermining the values that strengthen our society and our families. These families felt that their personal philosophies of child development called for a more responsive, positive environment than their local schools provided.

A small number of families were drawn to home schooling because they felt that the schools do too much to indoctrinate children in a progovernment, liberal mindset. They wanted to keep their children out of government-run institutions.

Another small group chose to educate their children at home because it was geographically inconvenient to attend school daily. They lived on remote farms or in mountain villages, or in foreign countries. Or the child had a physical handicap that made travel difficult.

But the largest and the fastest-growing group of parents joining the ranks of happy home schoolers are those who are appalled at the continuing collapse of public school education. They have no philosophical ax to grind; they simply don't want their children enrolled in third-rate schools.

Robert's parents fall into the last group. They didn't want to change the world, they only wanted to save Robert from a teacher who was destroying his natural curiosity and love of learning, from a school that cared more about classroom management than education, and from a district bureaucracy that cared more about maintaining inertia than stimulating learning. When they, as parents, realized that they were the only people in the world who really cared whether Robert learned anything, they felt they had no viable alternative but to teach Robert themselves.

And the fact that Robert's mother wasn't a real teacher turned out to be a benefit, not a deficit. In the public schools, the main job of a "teacher" is to manage a classroom; it's not important whether anyone learns anything in that classroom or not. Since Robert's mother had no classroom to manage, she didn't need all that teacher training and credentialing. She was free to be Robert's tutor, facilitator, guide, and caring resource. And if she wasn't as skilled as a certified teacher, she was a lot more responsive. In the classroom, Robert had less than ten minutes per day of direct teacher-to-Robert interaction. At home, Robert could have as much attention as he needed.

SOME COMMON MISCONCEPTIONS

"Home school kids are socially stunted."
"Home school kids don't learn as much."
"There are laws against home schooling."

A lot of misinformation has been circulated about home schooling, some of it by advocates of the established education system, who feel that their monopoly is threatened by the spread of home schooling. They try to paint this educational method, the one that educated all this nation's Founding Fathers, as an aberration by fringe cultists raising semiliterate social misfits. The home schoolers' response to this disinformation is, "Consider the source and look at our results."

That ordinary parents like Robert's mother aren't adequate substitutes for "qualified" teachers is a misconception so widely held that researchers in several states set out to prove it. Their intention was to use the results as an argument against home schooling. What they found, however, is that there is *no* relationship between the teaching certificate and student achievement. In the face of evidence to the contrary, it is dishonest for some states to continue insisting that only a credentialed person is capable of teaching.

Another misconception about home schooling is that children do not achieve as much if they are educated anywhere other than the traditional classroom. As in the example above, states have funded research in efforts to try to prove this hypothesis. What the studies proved was that home schoolers score far *above* their local schools in achievement. If we were to draw logical conclusions from the research, we would conclude that the schools should be shut down and *all* students should be taught at home.

Certainly everyone has heard that home schoolers are socially deprived. This assumption is based on the current social practice of schools—children should be segregated into packs of exactly the same age where they can compete for dominance and territoriality like wild animals; and they should do it without older role models of the same sex (or find their social role models in television sitcoms and cop shows); and this is somehow a preparation for life. Actually, the home situation's mixture of ages and its hierarchical status system is a closer match to the real world. It is the school, rather than the home, that provides an unreal setting that has little semblance

to real life. One study concludes, "Regarding socialization, it appears that very few home-schooling children
are socially deprived. . . . Apparently, the research data
indicate that it is the conventionally schooled child who
is actually deprived."[1] Among other factors, home-
schooled children have greater self-confidence, maturity,
and stability than their traditionally educated peers.

And what about the long hours and grueling effort required of a parent who wishes to home school? Mothers
and fathers who educate their children report that home
schooling takes less time than one might expect, and that
parents don't have to devote five hours every day in order
to get optimal results. Just because a school takes all day
to get through two hours of work, that doesn't mean that
home schoolers must drag it out, too. Experienced home
schoolers find that two or three hours a day are plenty.
And if an interesting interruption occurs, it simply provides an opportunity to broaden the child's education.

A final and damaging misconception about home
schooling is that it is illegal. Some school districts happily
encourage this erroneous assumption, because they like
the tax money they get for each enrolled child. They may
even threaten home schoolers with charges of truancy,
neglect, and child endangerment. But these pompous officials are just making noises. They know from experience
that they cannot win a case; they make an empty threat,
the parent calls their bluff, and they fold. Home schooling
is legal in every state. Only the conditions for home
schoolers vary from state to state.

In some states, the parent can simply decide to teach
the child at home, and then proceed to do so; in other
states, the parent must notify the local school district
that the children are home-schooled. In some states, the

parents must register as a private school, a requirement that is not as complicated as it sounds. Often, it means nothing more than filing a one-page form and keeping track of attendance. A few states require that even home-schooled children be taught by a certified teacher, but rarely does the state specify how much of the teaching must be done by that person. Parents in those states comply with the law by having the educational program supervised by, and occasionally taught by, the certified person.

To ascertain the legal requirements in your own state, DO NOT contact your local school district first. These offices are notorious for disseminating selected truths, half-truths, or even outright lies. To get the most complete, current information on the subject of home schooling, I suggest that you contact the association of home schoolers in your state.

HELP FOR THE HOME SCHOOLER

For families who are just getting started at home schooling, or who are interested in finding out more about this viable option, there are some excellent books on the subject. Among the most readable is *Family Matters: Why Homeschooling Makes Sense,* by novelist David Guterson.

John Holt was a home schooling enthusiast who began his career as a teacher and evolved away from organized schooling much the way many parents have done. Among his books are *How Children Fail, How Children Learn,* and *Teach Your Own.*

I also recommend *The Relaxed Home School,* by Mary Hood, or *The Successful Homeschool Family Handbook,*

by Raymond and Dorothy Moore, the godparents of home
schooling with a Christian slant. For parents of older students, I suggest *The Teenage Liberation Handbook,* by
Grace Llewellyn.

Even more useful and more timely than the books on
this subject are some very informative periodicals. They
provide home schooling families with current information on materials and resources (including Internet resources), parent exchanges where home schoolers share
advice, lists of local support groups, addresses of national
organizations, and up-to-the-minute information on
changes in state regulations. There are dozens of periodicals available by mail (you'll find at least one for each
philosophical subgroup within the home schooling movement), but the largest are:

Home Education Magazine
   (the widest circulation for general audiences)
PO Box 108
Tonasket, WA 98855
509-486-1351

The Teaching Home
(the largest Christian magazine)
PO Box 20219
Portland, OR 97220–0219
503-253-9633

Growing Without Schooling
(founded by the late John Holt)
2269 Massachusetts Avenue
Cambridge, MA 02140
617-864-3100

Practical Homeschooling
(conservative Christian, with excellent reviews of
   materials and resources)
PO Box 1250
Fenton, MO 63026

There are specific home school organizations specifically for Catholic, Jewish, Muslim, Adventist, Mormon,
and other groups, but the largest national groups are:

National Homeschool Association
PO Box 157290
Cincinnati, OH 45215-7290
513-772-9580

National cHallenged Homeschoolers Associated
   Network (NATHHAN)
5383 Alpine Road SE
Olalla, WA 98359
206-857-4257; NATHANEWS@aol.com
This is the group for disabled and special ed home
   schoolers.

Moore Foundation
PO Box 1
Camas, WA 98607
360-835-2736

In addition to the national groups, there are hundreds
of local support groups covering every variation in religion and philosophy. In nonrural areas, a home schooling
family may have a choice of a dozen support groups.
You'll find a current list of the larger groups near you in
Home Education Magazine.

Curriculum and Correspondence Families who are new to home schooling are often looking for a program that replicates the regular school experience. They may expect the home schooling to be temporary, and assume that their child will return to the school system at some not-too-distant point. Typically, these families turn to an established correspondence school program, because it provides a complete packaged educational program by mail, including textbooks, curriculum, exercises, tests, interaction with teachers, and report cards.

The oldest and most academically respected correspondence program for elementary schoolers is the one developed by the Calvert School, 105 Tuscany Road, Baltimore, MD 21210. The standard for children of American diplomats posted to obscure points of the globe, and the program of choice for many concerned parents living beyond the proximity of quality schools, the Calvert School program has recently been adopted by one of Baltimore's inner-city schools . . . with remarkable results.

Clonlara School Home Based Education Program, 1289 Jewett Street, Ann Arbor, MI 48104, is another large and respected correspondence school that provides curriculum, texts, and interaction. The Moore Foundation is also large and well thought of. They use a variety of textbooks, allowing more flexibility than most correspondence schools.

There are many Christian correspondence schools, of which the largest is the A Beka Correspondence School, Box 18000, Pensacola, FL 32523. They provide curriculum and support with a religious viewpoint. Among Catholic home schoolers, the Seton Home Study School, 1350 Progress Drive, Front Royal, VA 22630, is popular.

Families that begin home schooling often find that

their children make so much progress, both academically and personally, that they wouldn't dream of returning them to an organized school setting. As they become more comfortable with the theory and practice of home schooling, they tend to drift away from a structured correspondence school model and shift to a program that allows for greater self-direction without teacher-by-mail support. As their children become more and more self-motivated, they are allowed to direct their own learning and, in effect, create their own personal curriculum. Free from the structures of a set program, they can follow their own unique interests and talents. In such cases, textbooks become less important; educational supply stores, catalogs, bookstores, and libraries become the resources of choice. The children work harder than ever, but they don't think of it as work.

There is a small percentage of families who carry this pattern to its extreme. They become what is known in educational lingo as "unschoolers." The unschoolers believe that a child learns what he needs to know of life through apprenticeship, and that a boy or girl who learns to be an adult by modeling after adults will learn valuable lessons that he or she could never learn in a classroom. Unschoolers reject anything that smacks of traditional education, including textbooks. Math and history are taught only as needed and only when the child is motivated to learn these subjects.

Although the unschoolers are often presented as a caricature by critics who want to portray all home schoolers as extremists, this splinter group represents the far end of the range of home schoolers. It does not represent the million home-schooled children who are currently exceeding national norms in achievement.

What the Well-Educated Child Needs to Know

If your child is stuck in a class with a bad teacher, he still needs to learn the appropriate content for his grade. If the bad teacher isn't doing the job, *you* will need to teach him; what does he need to know? And if you give up on the schools altogether and decide to home school your child, what do you need to teach him? You will be amazed how little you need to do to outperform your local school.

Seventh grade teachers at several top private schools were asked, "What do you expect children to know when they come to you?" In other words, what *should* children have learned in their entire six years of elementary school? The response from the top schools was this: Students should be able to add, subtract, multiply, and divide—with whole numbers, fractions, and decimals. They should be able to understand what they read, and should be able to write complete sentences that are organized into paragraphs.

That's it. That's all. It doesn't seem a lot to ask from six years of school, but think about it. The presumption is that if kids can do these things, they can quickly learn the less important things. The secondary schools are confident that they can teach students to punctuate, capitalize, and do geometry. They also assume that any child with a sense of wonder and an inquiring mind has learned more science and social studies outside the classroom than in it.

Is it really as simple as that short list implies? It is . . . with some qualifications.

In math, the most important thing an elementary school child needs is to understand the structure of the number system. Does the child know that the fourth place over is always the thousands place? Can he write the number three million seventy-five thousand six as 3,075,006 with all the zeroes in the right places? Can he count backward from 10,012 to 9,998 accurately? Children who can't perform these exercises are trying to make sense of a number system where numbers fluctuate wildly in value and have no fixed relationship to each other. I have found that this problem—the lack of understanding of the structure of our number system—is the main cause of poor math performance in fifth through eighth grade.

The other fundamentals that primary school children need are memorized knowledge of addition and subtraction combinations and, in the middle-upper elementary grades, memorized knowledge of the multiplication tables. Everything else are details that can be picked up quickly in junior high if not learned in elementary school.

In reading, the criterion for success is simple: Does the child understand what he reads? And, as in math, it takes some groundwork to get to the level of true comprehension.

In kindergarten, reading comprehension means *understanding the meaning of a letter*—that it stands for a particular sound. In first grade, reading comprehension means *understanding the meaning of a word*—that it stands for a particular object or concept. In the grades that follow, reading comprehension means *understanding the meaning of a sentence*. In the upper elementary grades, and on through high school, college, and graduate school, reading comprehension means *understanding the meaning of a paragraph*.

Some schools do a rotten job at both ends of elemen-

tary school. At the beginning, they fail to teach students
the meaning of the letter; that is, they fail to teach phonics. Researchers discovered years ago that the best readers don't use phonics. Instead, they read by sight. So the
researchers concluded that all children could become like
the best readers if they learned to read by sight—and the
"whole language" method was born. Unfortunately, researchers overlooked the fact that the best readers are
high-IQ kids at the top end of the bell-shaped curve, and
you can't generalize from the extreme end of the range;
those kids taught themselves because they are bright. Average kids can't learn to read the same way; they need to
learn phonics or they don't learn at all.

At the other end of elementary school experience, the
children should be taught to read one paragraph at a time,
to look for and identify the main idea of each paragraph.
That is what reading comprehension is for this age group.
Since everything the child does in school for the next ten
years depends on mastery of this one basic skill, one
would assume that the schools would spend lots of time
on it. But ask your child whether his school spends any
time on it at all. It's entirely possible he will tell you that
his reading lesson consists of reading short stories from
an anthology and then answering discussion questions
like, "How did Tigger feel when he bounced to the top of
the tree and could not get down?" They are interesting
questions and may promote enjoyment of literature, but
they have nothing to do with reading comprehension.

Throughout the elementary years, a child's reading
should develop in speed, vocabulary, and comprehension.
Many schools have developed or bought elaborate and expensive plans to improve these skills, but they rarely emphasize the only method proven to work: pure volume of

reading. I spent eight years evaluating math and reading programs for school districts that wanted to document progress so they could continue to get government funding. In all that time, I saw only three programs that actually *did* improve reading skills, and all three were programs that emphasized extensive volume of reading. Teaching comes out of a teacher's mouth, but learning occurs inside a child's head; and extensive reading makes more things happen inside the child's head than a teacher ever could.

In writing skills, the criterion again is quite simple: Can the child use the English language to communicate effectively? The keys to this skill are practice, practice, and practice. And in this area, too, the bad teachers fall down. The classes assigned to them are too large, and since the union contract says the teachers don't have to take work home with them, they don't assign enough written work because they don't want to grade the papers. So the children don't write enough to develop their writing skills. Is it any wonder that parents with no classroom teaching experience become confident, skillful home school teachers in no time flat? Is it surprising how little it takes to outperform the existing school system?

A recent critic of the educational establishment said, "The truth is that reading, writing and arithmetic only take about one hundred hours to transmit as long as the audience is eager and willing to learn."[2]

The Finish Line

Keep your eye on the finish line. When all the education is said and done, what kind of person do you want your child to be? And how do you help your child reach that finish line? These are things that *you* must do:

1. Find the right school and teacher.
2. Make sure the teacher is sensitive to the needs of your individual child.
3. Defend and support your child if he has a bad teacher.
4. Find and treat learning problems, or share information so that experts can do so.
5. Ensure that the child acquires the important values, skills, and knowledge.

You are the only person in the world who really cares whether your child learns anything, so you must take the responsibility for your child's education. If your child has a bad teacher, *you* must do something, because no one else will. This book has told you that you can't depend on the teacher because:

- the teacher may *be* the problem
- the teacher may not be smart enough to diagnose or solve the problem
- the teacher may be too busy to solve your child's problem. He has other priorities with stronger claims on time.

You can't expect help from the principal, because she may be unwilling or unable to help you. She, too, has other priorities that outrank the needs of your individual child. The district, the private school, and the church school may not provide the ideal solution for your child. In the end, it comes down to you alone.

I hope this book has helped you to see the finish line and how to get your child there. Perhaps it has helped you find a way to get more from your child's teacher, or to diagnose and solve problems. Perhaps it has helped you get your child transferred to a better classroom, or school, or district. If nothing else has worked, it should be perversely reassuring for you to know how little schools teach anyway—that if the schools don't care whether your child learns anything, you can teach her the important skills yourself.

Your child's education is too important to leave in the hands of the schools. Don't let bad teachers or bad schools stand in your way, or distract you from the finish line. Your child's future depends on *you.*

Endnotes

The author regrets the nonexistence of more recent publications and hopes this book will shed some light on the often neglected (perhaps forbidden) topics of teacher quality and its effects on children.

CHAPTER 6

1. William A. McCall and Gertrude R. Krause, "Measurement of Teacher Merit for Salary Purposes," *Journal of Educational Research,* p. 73, 53: Oct. 1959.
2. V. S. Vance and Phillip C. Schlechty, "The Distribution of Academic Ability in the Teaching Force," *Phi Delta Kappan* 64: Sept. 1982; also Weaver, W. Timothy, "In Search of Quality . . . ," *Phi Delta Kappan* 61: Sept. 1979.
3. Perry, quoted in Donna Kerr, "Teaching Competence and Teacher Education in the United States," *Teachers College Record,* p. 529, 84: Spring 1983.
4. Phillip C. Schlechty and V. S. Vance, quoted in Donna Kerr, ibid.
5. Richard Mitchell, "Testing the Teachers: The Dallas Experiment," *Atlantic,* p. 66, 242: Dec. 1978.
6. Perry, op. cit.
7. Arthur Jersild, *When Teachers Look at Themselves,"* Teachers College, Columbia University, 1955.
8. Ibid.
9. William A. McCall and Gertrude R. Krause, op. cit.
10. Eric Hanushek, *The Value of Teachers in Teaching,* Carnegie Corp. and Rand Corp., Dec. 1970.

CHAPTER 12

1. John Taylor of Andrews University, quoted in the California Homeschool Network Information Packet, 1996.
2. John Taylor Gatto, *Dumbing Us Down: The Hidden Curriculum of Compulsory Schooling* (Philadelphia: New Society Publishers, 1972).